THE FIRST SUPPER

A COLLECTION OF STORIES AND RECIPES FROM THE REFUGEE WOMEN OF MEMPHIS
COMPILED BY CATHOLIC CHARITIES REFUGEE SERVICES

First Edition 1997

ISBN 0-9659923-0-6

PHOTOGRAPHIC CREDITS ——————————————————————————————

Charlie Binkowitz, Unicorn Graphics
4, 9, 12, 18, 24, 27, 32, 38, 41, 42, 46, 48, 61, 66, 70, 71

Alejandra Briseno
51, 56

Amy Brown
57

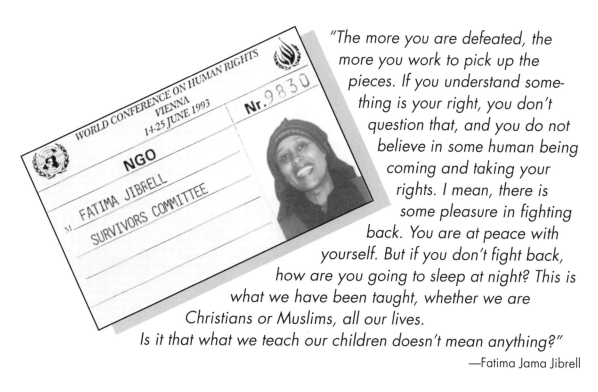

"The more you are defeated, the more you work to pick up the pieces. If you understand something is your right, you don't question that, and you do not believe in some human being coming and taking your rights. I mean, there is some pleasure in fighting back. You are at peace with yourself. But if you don't fight back, how are you going to sleep at night? This is what we have been taught, whether we are Christians or Muslims, all our lives.
Is it that what we teach our children doesn't mean anything?"

—Fatima Jama Jibrell

**THIS BOOK IS DEDICATED TO FATIMA JIBRELL,
WHO WENT BACK TO HELP THOSE WHO STAYED BEHIND.**

Acknowledgements

We would like to thank—

JANE EVERSHED, for so graciously allowing us to use her beautiful art on our cover, and for giving us her words, especially the title; they have been our constant inspiration;

ELLEN ROLFES, for believing in our project from the very beginning;

CHRISTI SHAW and LARRY COPPOCK, for their guidance and handholding;

PAULA CASEY, for infusing us with energy when we really needed it;

CHARLIE BINKOWITZ and Unicorn Graphics, for stepping in at precisely the right moment;

ALICE HARDY and CONNIE HOFFMAN, two of the best cooks we know, for proofing the recipes;

ERIN BLAND, ROBIN MARVEL, NETTIE SMITH, and NETTIE STROCKBINE for proofreading *ALL* of it;

And *THE FIRST SUPPER COMMITTEE* for their support and hard work.

We would especially like to thank all the women who fed us and shared their stories with us. This book is our tribute to their graciousness and courage.

JANE EVERSHED'S STORY

When I was nine years old, my family left England on a six-week ocean liner voyage. Our destination: South Africa. We disembarked into a separate world. A closed-off white enclave from which I would emerge years later in horror. I was so sheltered, I had never even heard of the African National Congress (ANC) until I left school. In my early twenties, I volunteered to teach art to Zulu children. Each week, I crossed through distinct racial borders, a Nazi palette of urban planning and control known as apartheid. As a white person, I knew I was inextricably a party to the brutal oppression of a people who couldn't even move freely in their own land. This realization was a cathartic turning point in my life and was the primary catalyst for my work as a socially conscious artist.

After the birth of my son, I decided we should leave the country. At that time it was mandatory for white males to serve in the South African Army, so to stay was to commit his future to white supremacism. Also, I had been jailed once for activism and, given my political stance, I was certain it would happen again. I realized, therefore, that I could be more effective furthering the cause of freedom from outside the country. My very first paintings, the *Dream for South Africa* series, expressed a vision of peace and justice for the land I loved, but could no longer rightfully call my home. Years later I realized racism is everywhere; white South Africa just gave it an official name—apartheid.

In 1984, when I was 25 years old, my son and I came to live in Minnesota with his father. The long, dark winters were a brutal shock compared to the warm, subtropical climate in which I had grown up. I was far from family and friends and felt desperately alone. As a homebound housewife and now mother of two, it became clear that the career of the man of the house took precedence over mine. Here *my* freedom was at stake, yet I refused to surrender my spirit. My only outlet from the never-ending monotony of domestic duties and society's expectations of women was my art. Guided by the flying women that emerged in my paintings, I began to soar, invoking new heights of consciousness through my *Power of Women* series.

Another series, *You and I, We are the Majority,* voiced the parallels I saw between that of African people and that of women worldwide. Exploring deeper into the domination of women, I then realized that this same mindset is responsible for the rapacious violence against nature. My reaction to these injustices resulted in the *Scarred Sacred Earth, Animals Crying,* and *Realm of the Nurturing Man* series.

I am convinced that when we as women reclaim our full ancient powers, and when men awaken to their loving and caring nature, a balanced society respecting all life is truly possible. My work stands in affirmation of this belief.

Inspiring art wares available from Jane Evershed include note cards, journals, Jane's colorful book, a CD, large prints, and more. For a catalog, send $2.50 to P. O. Box 8874, Minneapolis, MN 55408.

JANE'S RECIPE

JANE'S WILD PEAR RIDE
BRITISH, SOUTH AFRICAN, MINNESOTAN COMBO!

INGREDIENTS:

- 2 Cups Wild Rice
- 2 Pears
- 1 Onion
- 5 Cloves of Garlic
- 1 Tin Black Beans
- Sprinkle of Nutmeg
- Thumb of Ginger
- Sprinkle of Marjoram
- 1 tsp. Capers
- 3 tsp. Water
- 1 tbsp. Almonds

DIRECTIONS:

Place wild rice on the boil. Don't forget about it.

Sauté onions and garlic until slightly burnt. Add black beans (pre-cooked!).

Add chopped pears and spices, nutmeg, ginger and marjoram.

Add a knifeful of Capers.

Add 3 teaspoons of water.

Simmer and cover long enough to heat thoroughly.

Spoon over the rice. Add sliced almonds.

Enjoy!

THE FIRST SUPPER
STAFF

EDITOR
Judy Powell

**STORIES/RECIPES
GATHERING AND EDITING:**
Stacey Greenberg
Alejandra Briseno

SPANISH TRANSLATIONS
Alejandra Briseno

PHOTOGRAPHY
Charlie Binkowitz, Unicorn Graphics
Amy Brown
Alejandra Briseno

FRONT COVER ART & CONCEPT
Jane Evershed

ILLUSTRATIONS
Jennifer Rossi

GRAPHIC DESIGN
Paula May

PROMOTIONS MANAGEMENT
Jennifer Pack

TABLE OF CONTENTS

THE WORLD

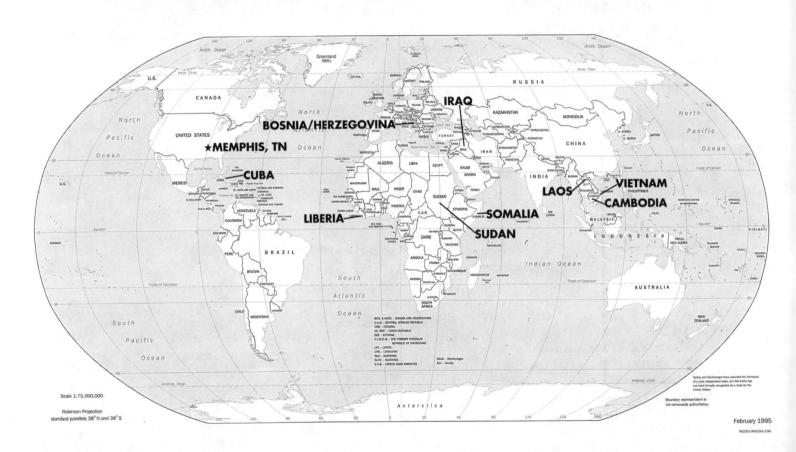

THE WORLD

IRAQ

RUSSIA

KAZAKHSTAN

MONGOLIA

BOSNIA/HERZEGOVINA

CHINA

★MEMPHIS, TN

CUBA

LAOS   VIETNAM

CAMBODIA

SOMALIA

LIBERIA

SUDAN

BOS. & HERZ. - BOSNIA AND HERZEGOVINA
C.A.R. - CENTRAL AFRICAN REPUBLIC
CRO. - CROATIA
CZ. REP. - CZECH REPUBLIC
EST. - ESTONIA
F.Y.R.O.M. - THE FORMER YUGOSLAV
         REPUBLIC OF MACEDONIA
LAT. - LATVIA
LITH. - LITHUANIA
SLO. - SLOVENIA
SLOV. - SLOVAKIA
U.A.E. - UNITED ARAB EMIRATES

Mont. - Montenegro
Ser. - Serbia

Scale 1:75,000,000

Robinson Projection
standard parallels 38° N and 38° S

Serbia and Montenegro have asserted the formation
of a joint independent state, but this entity has
not been formally recognized as a state by the
United States.

Boundary representation is
not necessarily authoritative.

February 1995

802353 (R00393) 2-95

INTRODUCTION

In the pages that follow, twenty-eight women tell you their stories and share their recipes with you. Some lived in villages in the jungle, some in big cities at the edge of a desert; some tended livestock, some earned college degrees and traveled abroad.

Yet no matter where or how they lived, all twenty-eight of them come from a war. They are survivors, women of courage, who agonized with their families over the decision to leave behind the countries that they love to come to a new world.

In these pages, they share with you their stories and, in so doing, affirm their lives and the choices that have brought them here. Whether they have been here 22 days or 25 years, they are all still homesick. They miss the family members they left behind, a way of life that will never come again. And yet they all celebrate the freedom that they have found here, even when it seems strange to them. Many speak of how they are different from American women, how much more freedom we have. And it is true. We are so fortunate, we think, as we listen to their words. For some of these women, we are the future—they will not live lives like ours. It is their daughters who will reap the ultimate benefit of their journeys to America. They will all go to school. They will all speak English. And they will all have the freedom to choose the lives they lead.

Yes, within these pages, freedom is celebrated. And more than that. For along with women's stories must always come the food. It has forever been women's work to feed their families, to nourish and celebrate life even in the midst of the dark days of war, and to pass on this legacy to their daughters. At the First Supper they were there, sisters in a circle, laughing, telling stories, sharing in the feast.

With this book, we issue you an invitation to join our circle.

Judy Powell
Refugee Services

SOUTHEAST ASIA

The refugees from the three southeast Asian countries of Cambodia, Laos, and Vietnam are the ones we at Refugee Services have come to know the best, in many ways, because we have known them the longest. The end of their war in 1975 marked our program's beginning and, even now, in 1997, we are still welcoming a few Vietnamese families to Memphis.

The people from these three countries are very different from each other, and yet have much in common. Their languages are very different, with each having a different alphabet. In fact, there are over 16 major languages spoken, and dozens of dialects. Their religions are also varied, with Buddhism and Catholicism being the two predominant religions of newly arrived refugees.

However, it is what the Cambodians, Laotians, and Vietnamese have in common that has come to have lasting meaning for the Refugee Services staff: their respect for elders and the primary, vital importance of family in the life of the community; the fundamental pursuit of peace and harmony in all aspects of life; and, of course, the important role that food and hospitality play in the cultures of all three countries.

Although some southeast Asians eat with chopsticks, some with knife and fork, and some with only a spoon, all enjoy rice as the staple food in their diets. Even in this most basic element, however, there is variety.   One of the liveliest discussions in the women's English class involved a debate about the best kind of rice and how to cook it!

The recipes that follow will give you some idea of the richness of the cuisine the southeast Asians have brought to Memphis. The stories that follow will give you a glimpse into the richness of their lives and the importance of memories, despite the passage of time.

CAMBODIA

CLIMATE

Tropical; rainy, monsoon season (May to Nov.); dry season (Dec. to Apr.); little seasonal temperature variation

COMPARATIVE AREA

Slightly smaller than Oklahoma

TERRAIN

Mostly low, flat plains; mountains in southwest and north

POPULATION

Total Population – 10,861,218

0 - 14 years	– 45%
15 - 64	– 51%
65+	– 4%

LIFE EXPECTANCY

For the Total Population	– 49.86 years
Males	– 48.39 years
Females	– 51.39 years

RELIGION

Theravada Buddhism 95%, other 5%

LANGUAGES

Khmer (official), French

COMMUNICATIONS

Number of telephones – 7,000

Number of radios – Number Not Available

Number of televisions – 70,000

SOPHAN LACH

Sophan Lach and her family came to the United States, to Memphis, in 1976, one year after the end of the war in southeast Asia. She was sixteen that year, old enough to be sad at having left behind the country she loved, young enough to consider each day in her new home an adventure. Her oldest sister, Saroeun, is the cook in the family, and the recipes included here are hers. Sophan explains that this is true for many Asian families, that the oldest daughter takes over the cooking and helps to care for the other siblings, even her older brothers. Saroeun has always been a wonderful cook, Sophan says, and Thanksgiving at her house is always the best!

SOPHAN'S STORY

I miss Cambodia a lot. My family and I used to live in the jungle. It was such a nice piece of land. We always saw all kinds of wild animals. I considered the wild animals as our neighbors since we lived so far away from other people. Before the war, I remember always getting up early to look at the sunrise. It was so beautiful. The sun would peek through the mountains nearby. As I sat and watched, my mother would bring me a bowl of rice. After sunrise, I was off. I would always go out into the open land and explore. I really miss those beautiful sunsets and mountains. I told my aunt to take a picture of a sunset for me. My aunt says she will not, because I need to visit her and see it for myself.

I can also remember the times we did not have shoes. If someone did, it was a luxury. It was awful having to walk around barefoot, because the grass in the jungle felt like metal. In order to have money, my father and older sisters had to get jobs. We also had to leave our home in the jungle and move into the village. That is when our problems began. My father did not get along with any of the village people. We had such big problems that we had to leave in the middle of the night. I remember my mother coming to wake me up and telling me we had to leave. I could not see anything since it was so dark, and I did not think my father knew where we were going. However, he knew exactly where he was taking us.

When we finally got into the city, it was daylight. I did not know how we were going to survive because we had no money or food. My father, however, was a very good engineer, so he later joined the army. The American Embassy realized that he was the best mechanic in the city, so they hired him. Since he now worked for the embassy, we were allowed to move to Thailand. We lived there for three years, hoping that Cambodia would get back to normal, but it got worse and worse. We were given the choice to take refuge in France or the U.S.. We decided to go to the U.S..

When we arrived in the U.S., everything was so new and exciting! It was hard for my parents, but for me and my siblings every day was an adventure. My parents had a hard time, because it was hard for them to learn English. My siblings and I always had to translate for my parents. It was easier for us to learn how to speak and write English. After I learned how to read, I read everything in sight. I took the GED and passed it. I was so proud of myself. I felt that I had finally made it. I always argue with my nephew, because he always complains about having to study and how hard it is for him. He doesn't realize the opportunities he has with his education and how hard it is working.

SAROEUN'S RECIPES

Our traditional Cambodian cooking has changed somewhat since we have moved to the U.S.. We still cook many typical Cambodian dishes, but my sister is very inventive with her cooking. She can create new dishes. We have also added U.S. national holidays into our family. For the traditional holiday meals such as Thanksgiving, we add quite a bit of our own ethnic food, such as rice or noodles. However, the people who cook the meals are still very traditional.

It is always the Cambodian women who cook and live in the kitchen. The men are too lazy to cook! The men are always in the living room or den. It is just like our religious praying, where women are on one side of the room and the men are on the other side of the room. I'm trying to break the cycle with my sister's son. I've told my sister that she needs to put him in the kitchen!

STUFFED CHICKEN WINGS

INGREDIENTS:

SEE INTERNATIONAL MARKETS ON PAGE 78 FOR ALL STARRED (*) INGREDIENTS

20 chicken uncooked wings
1 lb. ground turkey
3 leaves of wrinkled lime*, ground
2 garlic cloves, crushed
1 teaspoon MSG
1/5 teaspoon turmeric
1 package of vermicelli noodles, soaked in water for 10 minutes, then cut into small pieces
Salt and sugar to taste

DIRECTIONS:
Wash chicken wings, remove bones, leaving skin intact, and put them aside. Mix all ingredients together by hand until mixture resembles hamburger meat. Carefully fill each skin with the mixture, close, then place on a foil covered rack in a 300°oven for 30 to 45 minutes.

COCONUT POTATO CAKE

INGREDIENTS: 1 lb. raw shredded potatoes
6 eggs, beaten
1 cup sugar
11/2 cups canned coconut milk
3 tablespoons raw, unsweetened coconut

DIRECTIONS:
Mix all ingredients together and blend on high in a mixer for 10 minutes.

Pour into a deep pot and cook on medium heat, stirring often, until mixture becomes thick.

Then pour into a baking pan and cook at 350° for 20 to 25 minutes.

LAAP (GROUND MEAT SALAD)

INGREDIENTS:
1 lb. of ground meat
1/2 cup carrots, cut into thin
　matchsticks
1/2 cup cabbage, cut into 1/2"
　strips
1 shallot, minced
1 tablespoon fish sauce*
Juice of 1 lime
1 tablespoon sugar
1 tablespoon cilantro, chopped
1 tablespoon roasted rice (cooked
　rice, browned and blended)

DIRECTIONS:
Bring a big pan of water to a boil. Add meat, stir quickly, and remove when cooked.
Put drained meat in a wok on medium heat and add roasted rice. Add the sugar and the fish sauce, then stir. Add carrots, cabbage, and shallot. Next add the lime juice and mix well. Add the chopped cilantro and serve immediately.

CAMBODIAN CHICKEN SALAD

INGREDIENTS:
1 small chicken
1 medium onion, white or red
1 head of cabbage
3 - 4 cloves garlic
3 tablespoons of fish sauce*
1/2 cup mint leaves
Juice of 2 - 3 lemons
Sugar, salt, and ground peanuts to taste
Optional: cilantro and chili pepper to taste

DIRECTIONS:
Boil chicken until tender. Slice meat into small pieces after cooling.
Finely slice onion and cabbage, then mix with the chicken. Add mint.
In a separate bowl, mix the fish sauce and lemon juice together, then add sugar and salt to taste. Add garlic and chili peppers. Let sauce stand until ready to serve.

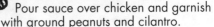

Pour sauce over chicken and garnish with ground peanuts and cilantro.

COMPARATIVE AREA
Slightly larger than Utah

CLIMATE
Tropical monsoon; rainy season (May to Nov.); dry season (Dec. to Apr.)

TERRAIN
Mostly rugged mountains, some plains and plateaus

POPULATION
Total Population – 4,975,772

0 - 14 years	*– 45%*
15 - 64	*– 51%*
65+	*– 4%*

LIFE EXPECTANCY

For the Total Population	*– 52.69 years*
Males	*– 51.14 years*
Females	*– 54.31 years*

RELIGION
Buddhist 60%, animist and other 40%

LANGUAGES
Lao (official), French, English, and various ethnic languages

COMMUNICATIONS
Number of telephones – 6,600
Number of radios – 560,000
Number of televisions – 32,000

Ta Rasasack (whose "real" name in Lao is Salysanh, which means 'city of peace') has been on the staff of Refugee Services for eight years now. He came to the United States in 1978 when he was 16 years old. His father remained in a prison camp until 1992, when he was finally released by the Communist government in Laos and allowed to join his family here in Memphis.

Ta's wife Davy came to the U.S. in 1978 also, the oldest daughter in a family of nine. She lived in Illinois, Oregon, and Louisiana before finally making her home here in Memphis with Ta.

The following story about the Laotian New Year is told by Ta.

NEW YEAR IN LAOS

The Laotian word for new year is Troot Songkan. The customary celebration lasts three days in April. The story behind the New Year revolves around a wealthy couple who had no children. They lived next door to a poor alcoholic who had two children.

One day the poor man went to the home of the rich man, and he said, "Even though you are wealthy, I am wealthier than you because I have children. When you die, you can't take your wealth with you, and there will be no one to inherit your money." When the wealthy man heard this, he felt ashamed and sad. For three years he prayed to God, the sun, and the moon to send him a child.

When the Troot Songkan came, the wealthy man and his servants went to a big tree next to the river where many types of birds were nesting. He took rice, dipped it in water seven times, steamed it until it was cooked, then gave it to the spirit of the big tree. The wealthy man also had a grand festival so that many could worship the spirit of the big tree. During the festival, he was praying to the spirit, asking him to bless him

with a son. The spirit felt sorry for him. He flew up into the sky to see the spirit in charge of the children. A boy named Thammapala was sent to be born to the wealthy couple.

The man loved Thammapala very much. He built a seven story palace under the big tree for his son to live in. Here Thammapala learned the language of the nesting birds. He also went to school and learned many things. He taught religion to all people and became much like a god.

One day an older man, Maha Phomkabimlaplom, a former monk, challenged Thammapala. He asked him three questions, and Thammapala had seven days to figure out the answers. If, at the end of the seven days, Thammapala could not answer, he would have his head cut off. If he could answer, then the old man would lose his head.

After six days, Thammapala could not answer. Giving up, he walked deep into the forest, hoping to die without shame. He grew tired and stopped to rest under a tree.

A pair of vultures were in the tree. The female vulture

asked, "What are we going to eat tomorrow?" The male vulture replied, "We are going to eat Thammapala, because he will not be able to answer the quiz, and he will get his head cut off." The female vulture asked what the answers were, and her companion told her. Thammapala heard the answers, because he had learned the language of the birds as a child. He was very happy and went back home.

The next morning, he went to Maha Phomkabimlaplom and told him the answers. Maha Phomkabimlaplom admitted that the answers were right, and he summoned his seven daughters to cut off his head for all to worship. But he said,

"My head is very sacred. If my head is placed on the softness of the earth, the world will burn. If my head is held up to the sky, there will be no rain. If my head is thrown into the ocean, it will dry up. Because of this, take my head and parade around Samend, the special pole, for sixty minutes, then place it on the holy mountain, Kraibath. Each year, you have to take turns parading my head around the pole and sprinkling it with holy water."

The daughters did what they were asked. Now each year there is a queen for Troot Songkan named after one of Maha Phomkabimlaplom's daughters.

DAVY'S STORY

Living here in the U.S., we aren't as strict as with the traditional Laotian female and male roles. My mother now sits down to eat with my father. My grandmother, however, never ate until after my grandfather was through. They never sat together at the table. Some Laotian women still wait for their husbands to eat first. At times, we still eat on the floor. When we are with our parents, we always eat in the traditional way.

Laotians are very superstitious. For example, the baskets that are used to make sticky rice can never be thrown away, even if they are ugly. It is bad luck to throw them away. Also, the head is very sacred. If someone touches another person's head, it would bring them bad luck. When we cut our hair, we bury the hair by a tree. Every tree, especially a big tree, is supposed to have a ghost. The ghost either protects you or it is your enemy.

One thing that I don't like about the U.S. is that there is too much work! Americans just work, work, work! In our country, it isn't that way. First of all, we don't have to buy houses, because they are passed down from generation to generation. For cars, one always pays cash. Mostly everything is paid for by cash. Over here, everyone has credit cards.

Most foreigners have the wrong idea about America. They think it will be easy to find a job and earn money, and that there are no poor people. I was eight when I came to the U.S., and we lived in a trailer. All of our beds were on the floor, and I thought to myself, "This is a house?!" Not that we had a luxurious life in Laos, but I had an image of life in America like in a fairy tale.

CHICKEN EGGROLLS *(makes 25)*

INGREDIENTS:

5 boneless chicken breasts
1 head of cabbage, sliced
4 regular size carrots, chopped
2 celery stalks, chopped
1 onion, chopped
1 garlic clove, minced
3 teaspoons salt
2 tablespoons soy sauce
25 super thin spring roll shells
Oil for frying

DIRECTIONS:

Chop chicken and stir fry with soy sauce and salt. Add vegetables and egg.

When cooked, put 3 tablespoons of filling in each spring roll shell and roll up. (Turn shell so it is diamond shaped. Fold over the left and right side, then roll from the bottom.)

Deep fry and serve.

CHICKEN LAP

This dish is prepared for special occasions, like weddings. We use the term "lap," which means "to bring luck or money." For weddings, this dish is a must, because it is important to start a marriage with luck. If a Laotian wedding is on Saturday, the drinking starts on Friday and ends on Sunday. During the reception, the newlyweds must go to each guest and give him or her a shot of liquor. It is also a tradition that each guest makes a donation to the couple. Instead of presents, people usually give money.

Laotians love spicy food. For any kind of occasion, such as a wedding, the women who cook count the number of people attending and put in one pepper for each person. It doesn't matter how many. I've had one dish that had at least 100 peppers! —Ta

INGREDIENTS:
4 boneless chicken breasts, baked for 20 to 30 minutes at 350°
2 - 3 green onions
1/2 lime
3 teaspoons crushed red pepper
3 - 5 small chili peppers, chopped
4 teaspoons fish sauce*
1 teaspoon MSG or salt
1 teaspoon black pepper

Optional:
1 bunch fresh cilantro
1 handful fresh bean sprouts
1 handful fresh mint leaves

DIRECTIONS:

Cut chicken into small cubes, squeeze lime over chicken. Add spices, then cilantro, bean sprouts and mint. Toss well and enjoy with rice on the side.

If mixture is too dry, add chicken broth or hot water.

L isa came to the United States in 1983. At that time, her first name was Nang. When she became a citizen, she changed her name to "Lisa."

LISA'S STORY

When I moved to Memphis, I was nine years old. My parents arrived a few months before me and my sister because they wanted to get settled in. They were living in an apartment complex, which I thought was their house! I did not know it was just a building with different apartments. I had never seen anything like an apartment complex. So, when I first saw the complex, I was just very impressed and remember thinking what a big house it was compared to the small house we lived in in Laos!

Sometimes I think about the things I miss, such as the fruit and the weather. I do not like it when it gets cold. During winter, I always wish I were back home. The weather is so nice and warm throughout the whole year. It is very hard to find the fruit that we had in Laos. If we do find it, it is usually expensive and does not taste the same.

I do not know if there is a big difference between cooking in America and cooking in Laos. I did not learn to cook until I moved to Memphis. I was still too young to learn when I lived in Laos. The kitchen is a little different. We did not have a stove in our kitchen in Laos. A fire had to be built in order to cook. In order to get drinking water, we went to a well. Also, the kitchen and bathroom were separate from the house. It is funny how I begin to remember the little differences when I am asked to talk about it! For instance, I remember during the first few days in Memphis, my mother asked me to go grocery shopping for her. I could not really find any of the food I was used to eating. This was before the Laotian grocery store had opened. Things have changed quite a bit since I was nine. Now there are many Asian stores throughout the city.

My life in America is different from my life in Laos. However, there are still many traditions that we honor. One honored tradition is the blessing of a new house by Buddha before moving into it. A house must be blessed before moving in, so that there will not be any bad spirits or bad luck.

Even though I have lived in the U.S. longer than I lived in Laos, my family is still very traditional. The one thing that we do not do much is go out to eat, which I think is a very American thing to do. My family and I usually cook at home.

My husband and I go out to eat more than my parents, which is really not that often. We only go out to eat or to the movies on special occasions, like our anniversary. We mostly get together with our family during the weekends. The women enjoy getting together to cook and to talk often.

The one big difference I have noticed living here is the difference in the attitudes of American women and Laotian women. The traditional role for a Laotian woman is to be a mother and a wife. American women seem to concentrate more on their education before they even begin thinking about a family. For me, I got married when I was eighteen. I did not think much about getting married at a young age. However, many American women get married at a much older age.

Dating is very different between the two cultures also. Laotian women traditionally do not go out much. Even if a Laotian girl has a boyfriend, she is not allowed to go out with him. The boyfriend must come to the house in order to see his girlfriend. Since my parents are still very traditional, I was not allowed to go out on dates. My dates were basically sitting around with the family or watching TV with my parents in the same room.

A single Laotian woman can also not live by herself. She has to live with her family until she is married. American women always seem to want to move out of the house when they are old enough. That is fine for American women, since they are more independent. This is not my way of life. I have been taught to behave as a Laotian woman. I have spent most of my life in America, but I am still very Laotian. My parents have raised me the Laotian way, "our" way.

LISA'S RECIPES

BBQ SAUCE

INGREDIENTS:
Fresh ginger
Fresh garlic
Fresh lemon grass
2 tablespoons oyster sauce*
Pinch of MSG, sugar, and salt

DIRECTIONS:
Mash ginger, garlic, and lemon grass together.

Add MSG, salt, sugar, and oyster sauce.

Brush over meat and cook.

HOT SAUCE

INGREDIENTS:

 5 fresh chili peppers, red or green

 1 clove garlic

 Fresh cilantro

 3 tablespoons fish sauce*

 A pinch of MSG and sugar

 Juice of 1/2 lemon

DIRECTIONS:

Mash chili peppers, garlic, and cilantro together.

Add other ingredients.

Mix well.

LAOTIAN LO MEIN

INGREDIENTS:

 1 package of lo mein noodles*

 1/2 lb. cooked, sliced pork

 1 handful bean sprouts

 1 green onion, chopped

 1/4 cup sugar

 1 teaspoon oil

 3 tablespoons sweet black soy sauce*

 A pinch of MSG

DIRECTIONS:

Soak noodles in water until soft.

Mix sugar and oil on medium heat until dark brown.

Add pork and stir, then add noodles, MSG, and soy sauce.

Turn off heat, then add bean sprouts and onion.

STICKY RICE

Sticky rice is *the* Lao rice. It is shaped into bite-size balls and dipped into a variety of sauces, including the hot sauce featured on page 14. In Laos, sticky rice is the cheapest rice at the market. Here, it is more expensive, and still the favorite.

Sticky rice can be found at Asian grocery stores. [See our listings in the back!] It should be soaked in water for at least one hour before cooking. When sticky, put rice in bamboo holder and put 2 inches of water in a metal pot. Place bamboo holder in metal pot and cook for 15 minutes, then take the bamboo holder with both hands and flip entire rice ball over. Replace and cook for 5 more minutes.

STEW

INGREDIENTS:

1/2 chicken, chopped (beef or pork may be used)

Small can of coconut milk

4 cups water

1/4 cup red curry paste*

Fresh lime leaf*

MSG, salt, and sugar to taste

1 cup mushrooms

1 cup green beans

Small can of bamboo shoots

1 yellow onion, chopped

DIRECTIONS:

Put coconut milk in a pot and let boil.

Stir in red curry paste until mixture is red, then add water and bring to a boil again.

Add chicken and let cook.

Add MSG, salt, and sugar.

Turn off the heat, then add vegetables.

Serve with steamed rice.

COMPARATIVE AREA

Slightly larger than New Mexico

CLIMATE

Tropical in south; monsoonal in north with hot, rainy season (mid-May to mid-Sept.) and warm, dry season (mid-Oct. to mid-Mar.).

TERRAIN

Low, flat delta in south and north; central highlands; hilly, mountainous in far north and northwest

VIETNAM

POPULATION

Total Population – 73,976,973

0 - 14 years	– 36%
15 - 64	– 59%
65+	– 5%

LIFE EXPECTANCY

For the Total Population	– 67.02 years
Males	– 64.69 years
Females	– 69.48 years

RELIGION

Buddhist, Taoist, Roman Catholic, indigenous beliefs, Islam, Protestant

LANGUAGES

Vietnamese (official), French, Chinese, English, Khmer, tribal languages

COMMUNICATIONS

Number of telephones – 800,000
Number of radios – 7.215 million
Number of televisions – 2.9 million

CHRIS BYRD

Chris Byrd has been in the United States since 1975. She is a bilingual counselor with Memphis City Schools Bilingual Program and is actively involved in helping refugee children from all over the world make the adjustment to our school system.

CHRIS'S STORY

I left Vietnam in 1975. I was 23 years old. Unfortunately, I have not been back to visit my family. I do not know how people would react to me if I returned for a visit. I think I would feel uneasy if I did return, since most of my people would probably be upset with how I have changed. I really do not consider myself Vietnamese anymore. I am very Americanized in many ways. For example, many Vietnamese people would consider my opinions and views very liberal. As for me getting a higher education, they would consider that very odd.

I came to the U.S. because I wanted a better education. I wanted more than what Vietnam could offer. I have to thank my father for encouraging me to leave. While most Vietnamese parents encourage the traditional gender roles within their family, my parents encouraged me and my siblings to achieve more than what our culture thought we deserved. My father taught us to do all that we could. He wanted the best for us.

When I decided to come to the U.S., my parents wanted me to go. They told me not to look back and not to regret the decision I had made. I remember still to this day the moment before I stepped onto the ship in Saigon. I was a bit hesitant about leaving my family behind. My father, however, told me to go, because it was my chance to better myself. His last words to me were, "I will see you again." Unfortunately, I never got the chance to go back before my father died. My mother, two younger sisters, and younger brother still live in Vietnam.

I do not regret my decision though. My life has been enriched by moving to the U.S. I do not know who I would be if I had stayed in Vietnam. I wish more Vietnamese people would be given the chance to receive a higher education, especially the women. My hope would be that all Vietnamese women would be more independent. Vietnamese women tend to be more introverted and helpless. Their husbands are the more dominant in the household. I wish Vietnamese women would be more expressive with what they desire to do with their lives. Even if the man is wrong, a Vietnamese woman would never say, "This is right, and this is what we should do!"

I do not see any changes happening with my generation. The Vietnamese women who are around my age and are educated are not as independent as American women. The majority of American women are more independent and assertive. Vietnamese women say that their position in life is their fate, and it is what God wants. "I am his wife, and I must do what he wants." I hope the next generation will be more independent and assertive.

Thinking about Vietnam makes me miss my home a lot. I have many special memories about living in Vietnam. I can remember the special times during the summers I lived there. Every summer, my father would drive our family to the south side of Saigon, to a beach called Lunco. It was a very popular place. My father would rent a whole restaurant for our family, including aunts and uncles and their children. The owner of the restaurant would cook wonderful recipes that could not be found anywhere else. I always had such fun the summers we traveled down to Lunco.

Holidays such as Tet were a big event in my family. Tet is one of the biggest holidays in Vietnam. We celebrate it for up to two weeks. Tet is very special to Vietnamese people, because this is the period when everyone turns a year older. That is why when you ask Vietnamese people when their birthday is, they respond that they do not really know. We do not distinguish each of our birthdays. Everyone's birthday is Tet! It always takes place during our New Year.

The dates of Tet change every year, because we use a lunar calendar. It can fall anywhere between the first week of January and the last week of February. One dish that you will find in everyone's home is a pot roast cut into chunks, cooked to a caramel color, with onions and coconut juice. There is always plenty of food. We are also plentiful in friendship, wealth, and health.

The food is so delicious during this time. I miss all Vietnamese food. One can pretty much find just about everything here, except for some fruit. For example, you can only find thomthom once a year here. Most fruits are tropical, so you can only find them in tropical areas.

There are also differences in the kitchen itself. In Vietnam, we only cook on stoves. Most Vietnamese have stoves, but no ovens. That is why when you go visit a Vietnamese person's home here, the oven is full of pots and pans. It is used as a storage area!

CHRIS'S RECIPES

SAUSAGE AND CABBAGE SOUP

INGREDIENTS:
1 head of cabbage, chopped into bite-
   size pieces
1 lb. cajun sausage, sliced
1 large onion, chopped
1 large can of whole tomatoes
1 can of kidney beans
2 cups of water
Salt and pepper to taste

DIRECTIONS:

Brown onion and sausage, then mix all ingredients in a pot.
Cook on medium heat for 30 minutes.

THIT KHO HOT VIT
(SPICY PORK ROAST)

This dish is usually served during Tet. It is eaten with steamed rice, pickled leeks, and rice noodles. It has been served in Chris's family for three generations.

INGREDIENTS:
2 lbs. pork roast, cut into pieces 1" thick
1 dozen eggs, hardboiled
I onion chopped
4 cloves garlic, chopped
2 cans coconut milk
1/2 cup sugar
Fish sauce*, salt, and pepper to taste

DIRECTIONS:
Pour sugar in a deep pan and turn stove on high.
Allow sugar to become caramelized, but don't let it become too dark, or it will be bitter.

Add onion and garlic, then pork, then salt and pepper.
Let meat turn light brown, then add coconut milk and fish sauce.

Peel eggs and add to pork caramel.
Reduce heat to medium high and let simmer for one hour or until meat is tender.

BEEF SALAD

INGREDIENTS:
2 lbs. rump roast, sliced thin
5 green onions, cut into 1" pieces
4 cucumbers, peeled and thinly sliced
4 tomatoes, thinly sliced
5 limes, halved
2 tablespoons oil
2 - 3 tablespoons sugar

Salt, pepper, red pepper, and fish sauce* to taste

DIRECTIONS:
In a frying pan, heat oil on high.

Add cut green onions and sliced meat.

Turn occasionally until medium well, then add salt and pepper to taste.

Put tomatoes and cucumbers in a mixing bowl.

Add meat and red pepper.

Squeeze in the limes, add sugar and fish sauce.

Serve with steamed rice.

CUBA

Refugee Services has welcomed two waves of Cubans to Memphis since it began in 1975. The first wave arrived in 1980 as a result of the Mariel boatlift, which brought 125,000 Cubans to the United States. The second wave began arriving in August of 1995, in preparation for the closing of Guantanamo Bay in January, 1996. By the time the base was closed, we had welcomed over 200 new Cuban immigrants to Memphis. We have received only a very small number since then.

The two women whose stories follow led different lives in their native country, and they arrived here in Memphis at different times. However, their words tell us something of the ongoing struggle for freedom in the island country so close to our own, and their recipes allow us to share in their love of Cuban cooking.

COMPARATIVE AREA
Slightly smaller than Pennsylvania

CLIMATE
Tropical; moderated by trade winds; dry season (nov.-Apr.); rainy season (May - Oct.).

TERRAIN
Mostly flat to rolling plains with rugged hills and mountains in the southeast.

POPULATION
Total Population – 10,951,334

0 - 14 years	– 22%
15 - 64	– 68%
65+	– 10%

LIFE EXPECTANCY

For the Total Population	– 75.05 years
Males	– 72.71 years
Females	– 77.54 years

RELIGION
Nominally Roman Catholic 75% prior to Castro assuming power; Protestants, Jehovah's Witnesses, Jews, and Santeria are also represented.

LANGUAGES
Spanish

COMMUNICATIONS

Number of telephones	– 430,000
Number of radios	– 2.14 million
Number of televisions	– 2.5 million

CUBA

Nestora Barcon-Ortiz came to the United States, to Memphis, with her father in September of 1996. In Cuba, she was a medical technician.

NESTORA'S STORY

I have enjoyed living in Memphis very much. Life is more tranquil here. I do, however, miss Cuba very much. Everything is beautiful in Cuba. The beautiful beaches, nice people, and nice weather make Cuba very enjoyable. Always being surrounded by family made the hardships more bearable. Family is very, very important to us. By having my family near, they can help me solve any situation. Family is such a necessity for emotional support.

The way of life was very difficult in Cuba, though. There has been a constant battle with life because the government is very strict. A man and woman can choose the career path, but there are certain restrictions. In my profession, my annual income was never equivalent to what I deserved for my professional status. I, of course, did have a nice apartment. Here I just have the necessities, but I feel more comfortable. Life is more tranquil here. I realize that one has to work hard in order to succeed in life, but we are free to do and say whatever we want.

There are no limitations to food or clothing as there are in Cuba.

The one thing I have had problems with while living in Memphis for the past few months is trying to communicate with people. I am still taking English classes, so I know very little English. It is very frustrating when someone is speaking to me, and I can't respond back to them. I just hate standing there not being able to say anything to the other person.

The only thing I miss besides my family and friends is the food. I still am not accustomed to American food. I try to avoid it because it is so fattening. I think I have gained ten pounds since I have lived here in Memphis! I miss the sweets. Cubans love sweets. The sweets here are not quite the same. Cuban sweets are much sweeter. We love putting sugar into desserts and making them sweeter. Not many people can eat our candy, because it is too sweet for them. Even though we enjoy sweets, we do not have a weight problem. I have gained more weight here. There is junk food everywhere! There are no fast food restaurants in Cuba.

We take pride in our cooking. The cooking style is not any different, but we appreciate the work that it takes to prepare the food.

NESTORA'S RECIPES

FLATTENED BANANAS

INGREDIENTS: 2 bananas (peeled and frozen)

1 cup of oil

1/4 cup of sugar

DIRECTIONS:

Cut each banana into five or more pieces. Fry the pieces in lukewarm oil for 10-15 minutes. Remove them from the oil and sprinkle sugar on top. Using a paper bag, smash each piece so it is flat. Cool in the freezer, then serve.

CUBAN STYLE BEANS AND RICE

INGREDIENTS: 1 lb. rice, cooked

1/2 lb. black beans, cooked

1 head of lettuce

1 tablespoon of chili sauce

1/2 teaspoon cumin

1/2 teaspoon ground laurel leaves

1/4 teaspoon oregano

2-3 cloves of garlic, chopped

DIRECTIONS:

Puree lettuce, chili sauce, and other spices. Mix with beans and serve over rice.

FLAN

INGREDIENTS:

1 can condensed milk

1 can evaporated milk

3 eggs

1 teaspoon vanilla extract

1/2 cup sugar

Salt to taste

DIRECTIONS:

Heat sugar over medium heat until caramelized. Let cool until it begins to crackle, then pour them into a round cake pan and spread throughout. Mix the remaining ingredients and pour the into the round cake pan.

Now fill a separate bowl, which is larger than the cake pan, with 1/3 water. Place the cake pan in the bowl, then put both into the oven. Bake at 350° for 45 minutes.

Check to see if the flan is done by poking a hole in the top. If the toothpick comes clean, the flan is ready.

DORIS FIGUEREDO-HECHAVARRIA

Doris Figueredo-Hechavarria arrived here from Cuba in September, 1995, with eight other family members. Almost two years in the United States has not diminished her love for her home country or her celebration of the freedom she has found here in Memphis.

DORIS'S STORY

In my opinion, Cuban food is much richer than any other food. There is such a variety of food for different occasions. Everyone I know who has tried Cuban food loves it! There are many women that I work with who ask for Cuban recipes. The food is *muy sabrosa* (very tasty).

Black beans are a necessity in Cuba. We have many dishes that include black beans and rice. There are also songs about our food. There is a song about the banana dish. The song talks about how sweet the bananas are.

Cooking is very much appreciated in Cuba. All Cuban women must learn how to cook well. It is expected of them. A Cuban man wants a woman who can cook and keep the house clean.

I really miss Cuba. Most of my family is still living there. I enjoy living in Memphis, but it is hard. I am still learning to speak English. One has to learn English well in order to get around. It is a much easier life, however, than in Cuba. Cuba is a very tropical and beautiful country, but there is always a crisis. The country wants to give, but it just can't. I had a great job. I was a political lawyer. I enjoyed my work, but the salary was very low. It was not enough to live on. Things are not cheap in Cuba. The only thing that the government did well was offer a free education to everyone in Cuba. Since we do have free education, a great majority of people go on to a higher education. There are many doctors, lawyers, psychiatrists, etc. People are also allowed to choose their career path, but there are some restrictions, such as the government giving certain rules and regulations to certain jobs. People can not go against these rules because they can lose their jobs.

Even though my job here in Memphis is not what I would like it to be, I enjoy life more. I am not having to worry about keeping quiet when I disagree with certain matters. Here I can speak my mind. I could basically go outside and scream how horrible the government is if I wanted and not worry about people coming after me! In Cuba, no one has any freedom of speech. I have also enjoyed meeting new people. I have met a lot of people from Cuba as well. It is nice forming a relationship with people who have gone through or are going through the same transition of moving and leaving their lives behind in another country. My Cuban friends, who are women, have helped me a great deal.

CHICKEN WITH RICE

INGREDIENTS: 2 lbs. of rice, cooked

4 chicken breasts, baked and chopped

1 head of lettuce

2 chili peppers

Cilantro, cumin, oregano, garlic, laurel
leaves, all to taste

2 tablespoons of oil

DIRECTIONS:

Puree lettuce, chili peppers, and spices. Fry rice in oil, then add pureed mix and cook for 15 to 20 minutes on low heat. Mix with chicken and serve.

AFRICA

Refugee Services has been resettling refugees from the African continent for a number of years, beginning with the country of Ethiopia. Currently, we are welcoming people from the following three countries:

LIBERIA. At the end of 1996, approximately 755,000 Liberians were refugees, and an estimated one million were internally displaced. A civil war that began in late 1989 has resulted in thousands of civilians being killed and many more thousands fleeing their homes and their country to seek safety and peace.

SOMALIA. Since 1988, up to a half a million Somalis have died in civil war and factional fighting. We have been resettling Somalis since 1991, when the war there was the most severe. In 1992 - 93, the United Nations sent peacekeeping troops to Somalia to protect relief efforts. These troops were all withdrawn by early 1995. The civil war there continues. At the end of 1996, approximately 455,000 Somalis were refugees.

SUDAN. The cultural, political, and religious differences between northern and southern Sudan have resulted in conflict over a long period of time. Civil war has persisted for the last 13 years. The Sudanese refugees coming to Memphis, for the most part, are from the southern part of the country and are mostly Christians or practitioners of traditional religions. There were approximately 430,000 Sudanese refugees and up to four million internally displaced persons at the end of 1996.

The numbers are hard to read. So much of Africa is in turmoil. The refugees who have come to Memphis from there share a heritage of war. However, their stories, like their countries, are very different. Some come from rural areas, some from the cities; some are Muslim, some Christian. The women whose stories and recipes follow reflect and celebrate this diversity.

COMPARATIVE AREA
Slightly larger than Tennessee

CLIMATE
Tropical; hot, humid; dry winters with hot days and cool to cold nights; wet, cloudy summers with frequent heavy showers

TERRAIN
Mostly flat to rolling coastal plains, rising to rolling plateaus and low mountains in the northeast

POPULATION
Total Population – 2,109,789

0 - 14 years	*– 45%*
15 - 64	*– 52%*
65+	*– 3%*

LIFE EXPECTANCY

For the Total Population	*– 58.59 years*
Males	*– 56.05 years*
Females	*– 61.22 years*

RELIGION
Traditional 70%, Muslim 20%, Christian 10%

LANGUAGES
English (official) 20%, Niger-Congo language group (approximately 20 languages)

COMMUNICATIONS

Number of telephones	*– Less than 25,000*
Number of radios	*– 622,000*
Number of televisions	*– 51,000*

PAULINE GBEE

P auline Gbee arrived in Memphis with her husband and eight children in January, 1997. Both she and her husband were teachers before coming to the United States.

PAULINE'S STORY

C oming to Memphis was a big relief for me and my family. In my country, there is a horrible war going on, and the people are not free. The war is very hard to explain. The people are fighting among each other. It is more of a political war. One person says that we must do things this way, but another says that his political views are wrong. So another person decides to create a new political party because he disagrees with the current view. It is an outbreak. In a small country like Liberia, it is hard to escape the effects of the war. People are being hurt emotionally and physically.

Those who are being affected the most are the children. To grow up seeing people fight and die is just the worst environment for children. My children had a hard time adjusting, especially living in a refugee camp. Parents cannot choose the school they want their children to attend. There are a set of refugee schools that refugee children must attend. After high school, going to a higher level of education is also hard for the children because they must know French. Most of the schools in the refugee camp are not equipped to help a child move on to a higher education. The camp we were living in was fine. If you went outside the camp, the government did not have open arms to refugees.

I hope the war will end. My fear is that even if it does, there are still going to be a lot of problems. People are always being forced to take one side or another. There is no freedom. Unfortunately, my parents are still in Liberia. I would like to go back to visit them. For now, I want to make Memphis my home.

I have not had any problems adjusting to Memphis. It is not very hard for many Africans to adjust to living in America. Many of us do not live much differently than from the people here. There are many differences, but also some similarities. There are many Western customs in Africa. Like the weddings. Many women buy wedding dresses from America. Instead of having some of the African influence in a wedding, it is all European. I had a mixture of the European and African influences in my wedding. We did have rice and flowers thrown down the aisle, and a wedding cake as it is done in America. However, there were some traditional African elements. We had a girl holding a basket with different foods

like rice and sauce, which symbolizes that the woman will cook at all times for the family. Another girl carries a broom that represents that the wife will always keep the house clean, too! The groom carries a cow tail that represents that, as a husband, the man will always protect the wife.

African weddings are very colorful. All bridesmaids wear the traditional African dress, but each wears her own color. The groomsmen also wear the traditional clothing and coordinate their color with one of the bridesmaids.

For weddings, there are always friends who help. There are two sets of people who help prepare the wedding. One group of people are called the organizers. The organizers help the couple get everything ready for the wedding by providing financial support and getting the materials. There are also hostesses, who are responsible for the preparation of the food. Both groups are either family or friends. They also pay for everything. All the money used for the wedding come out of their pockets. This is an honored African tradition that helps the couple financially. Since the newlyweds are just beginning their new life, they should not be burdened with paying for a wedding. They start fresh soon after their marriage.

Another cultural difference is the age at which women get married. Girls can be as young as fifteen. Also, it is the man who picks his future wife. The women have no say in the matter of who they marry. There can be a huge age difference between the couple, but it does not matter, since the man can pick his wife to be as young as fifteen.

The one difference that my children have found difficult to adjust to is the weather. They do not like cold weather! My husband and I do not like winter time either. It always rains, too. In Liberia, it does not rain very much. If it does, it rains for maybe an hour. But, in that hour, it rains very hard. The majority of the time, the sun is out. One can always go out and walk. My children comment on how they never see anyone out in the streets walking. That is because they are in their cars! People do not have cars in Liberia. Everyone walks to their destination. During the weekend, you always see the kids outside playing. Everyone is always outside doing something.

Another difference between America and my home country is the cooking. The cooking style is different, since the kitchen is outside and not part of the actual house in Liberia. We use firewood in our kitchens. I have found it difficult to find some of the food that we ate in Liberia, such as palm oil, potato greens, and dried fish. If I do find them in a store, they are very expensive.

Since we have been in Memphis, my oldest daughter has been helping me quite a bit with the cooking. At around six years old, girls begin to learn how to cook. The mother is usually the one who teaches her daughters. My children always help me in the kitchen, even my sons. They are either helping me cook or helping me clean the dishes. During the weekend, my oldest daughter does most of the cooking. It is my time for a break. It also helps her prepare herself for what she must do in the future.

OKRA SAUCE WITH PALM OIL

INGREDIENTS: Meat, fish and chicken, cut into small pieces

2 to 3 cups okra, cut in thin rounds

2 large tomatoes, chopped (or 3 tablespoons tomato paste)

1 onion, chopped

1/2 cup palm oil* (or vegetable oil)

3 cups water

2 tablespoons meat tenderizer

1 teaspoon each — black pepper
ginger
poultry seasoning
season-all
red pepper
garlic powder
1/2 teaspoon salt
1 chicken bouillon cube

DIRECTIONS:

Wash meat thoroughly and season with red pepper, ginger, garlic powder, season all, poultry seasoning, and black pepper. Add meat tenderizer and let stand for 10 minutes. Set fish aside for frying.

Boil meat and chicken in water, adding 1 tablespoon of cut onions, and 1 teaspoon salt. Bring to a boil for 20 minutes to enable meat to be thoroughly done. In a separate pan, heat oil, then add fish. Fry until golden brown, then remove. Now fry the rest of the onions and tomatoes until tender, then add cut okra. Cover and stir occasionally to avoid burning. When okra is fried, add stock from meat and chicken, and add the bouillon cube. Let boil for about 10 minutes, then lower the heat and allow to simmer until all of the water cooks off. Remove from the heat, add meat, chickent and fish, and serve with rice.

FRIED POTATO GREENS

INGREDIENTS: 1 lb. meat of your choice (fish, beef, chicken, or pork)

4 bunches of potato greens (or other greens), thoroughly washed and drained

1 onion, sliced

1 large maggi cube* (bouillon may be substituted)

1 cup of oil

2 cups of water

Salt and red pepper to taste

DIRECTIONS:

Cut meat into small pieces and boil for 20-25 minutes with maggi, salt, and red pepper. Shred greens and fry with onions for 5 minutes. Stir to avoid sticking. When fried, add the stock from the meat and let boil until water is almost evaporated. Add meat and simmer for 5-7 minutes. Serve with rice.

COMPARATIVE AREA
Slightly smaller than Texas

CLIMATE
Principally desert; Dec. to Feb.–northeast monsoon, moderate temperatures in north and very hot in the south; May to Oct.–southwest monsoon, torrid in the north and hot in the south, irregular rainfall, hot and humid periods between monsoons.

TERRAIN
Mostly flat to undulating plateaus rising to hills in the north

POPULATION
Total Population – 9,639,151

0 - 14 years	– 44%
15 - 64	– 52%
65+	– 4%

LIFE EXPECTANCY

For the Total Population	*– 55.49 years*
Males	*– 55.18 years*
Females	*– 55.80 years*

RELIGION
Sunni Muslim

LANGUAGES
Somali (official), Arabic, Italian, English

COMMUNICATIONS

Number of telephones	*– 9,000*
Number of radios	*– 350,000*
Number of televisions	*– 113,000*

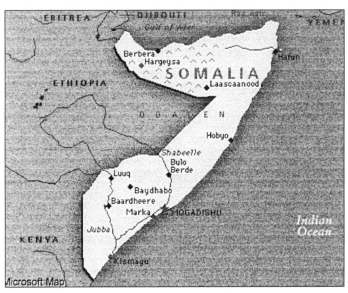

SOMALIA

FADUMA ASAD

*F*aduma and her family (including the granddaughter pictured with her here) resettled in Memphis in July of 1996. Faduma's husband, Sharif, now works on our staff at Refugee Services. Having the opportunity to share closely in this family's adjustment process has taught us so much about the courage and humor it takes to begin new lives in a new land.

FADUMA'S STORY

When I came here, I saw that American women had more freedom, much more than Somali women. Because when we go out, we have to cover ourselves with a long dress that covers from head to foot. When I came here, I tried to go out in the street in traditional dress, and everyone looked at me. And so I think American women are very different from Somalis, especially the way they move around and the way they dress.

I think the American family has very good customs, because the members of the family go to work, and they educate their children. They don't leave the children uneducated. They take much better care of education, which is different from our families. You will find that sometimes the children don't go to school, especially the girls.

They just stay at home, because the parents don't allow them to go.

I was brought up illiterate. I can't read and I can't write. The boys are sent to school, but the girls must stay in the house and help the mother and the other children. But I see that here you must educate your children. I have two children going to high school, and my son has two children going to elementary school. I learn from my husband. When he comes home, I say, "Teach me!"

A WORD FROM NAFISA, FADUMA'S DAUGHTER

I like living in Memphis. In Somalia, there was always fighting, and we didn't have a house. I miss Somalia, but there is nothing left for me there. I have been here seven months, and so far my favorite things are pizza and soap operas! I'm learning English from the television and Spanish from my sister's friends at school.

SAMBUSA (DEEP FRIED MEAT POCKETS)

INGREDIENTS:

1 - 2 lb. ground beef, browned and drained

1 large purple onion, chopped

3 tablespoons garam masala powder*

1 tablespoon black pepper

1 jalapeno pepper, diced

2 cloves garlic, finely chopped

1 tablespoon canola oil

Salt to taste

Oil for frying

DIRECTIONS:

Sauté onion in oil, then add other ingredients. Mix well.

Wrapper Ingredients:

3 cups flour

2 tablespoons canola oil

1/4 cup water

DIRECTIONS:

Mix ingredients in a bowl and knead into dough. Divide in 9 to 10 sections and roll into balls (should be about 2" in diameter). Roll each ball out into a flat circle about 6" in diameter. Make two stacks of four (or five), being sure to rub oil between layers to prevent them sticking together. Roll each stack out until circle has a diameter of 12". Cut each circle into four equal triangles.

Preheat pan on high. Add one triangle at a time. Let cook until it begins to bubble, then flip. Remove triangle and lower heat. Gently peel layers apart and set aside. If edges are crunchy, remove with a knife. Repeat with each triangle.

Assembly:

Mix flour and water in a bowl until pasty. Hold triangle in hand, pointing down. Rub paste on top right half along the edge. Fold left side down and rub paste on the edge. Fold right side down to meet left side and form a cone. Turn over and fill with one big spoon of meat mixture. Tuck short side in and paste long side down. End product should be a triangle! Repeat with others, then deep fry.

ANGEERA (FLAT BREAD)

Angeera is a flat bread, similar to a pancake, eaten with all meals, or at breakfast with honey.

INGREDIENTS: 2 cups self-rising flour

1 cup milk

1 egg

2 tablespoons sugar

DIRECTIONS:

Combine flour, egg, and milk in a large bowl. Add a little water to soften up the mixture and add sugar. Stir until soft. Put a frying pan on the stove and preheat it on high. If you don't have a seasoned pan, rub the pan with oil first. When the pan is hot, put 1/2 cup of the mixture in. When mixture begins to bubble, flip it over and cook on the other side. Remove. Continue cooking in this manner until all of the mixture is used.

SADIYO SHIRE

Sadiyo Shire arrived in Memphis in December of 1996 with her husband and four children. She speaks beautiful English and briefly worked part-time for Refugee Services as an interpreter. She wants, most of all, to continue her education.

SADIYO'S STORY

My mother taught me how to cook when I was ten years old. I like to cook. It is my birthright. A woman is supposed to cook. In Somali culture, the men don't know how to cook, so the women must. My daughters are still too young to help me in the kitchen. I will teach them when they are nine or ten.

The way I cook hasn't changed since I came to Memphis, but the food I cook is different from American food. For example, we eat angeera (flat bread) for breakfast. I like to try American food, but I'm not accustomed to it. My stomach rarely agrees with American food! One way that cooking is different here is that there are schools that teach people how to cook. In Somalia, there are no such schools! A woman learns how to cook through her family, her mother.

For special occasions, like weddings, a lot of women will get together and cook. Usually, fifteen or more women will cook for special celebrations. We cook mostly the same foods that we would eat any other day, but we make a lot more sweets than normal. Ramadan is also a special occasion when we cook special dishes.

American women and Somali women are different in terms of religion. Most Somali women are Muslim, and we tend to strictly adhere to Islamic beliefs. It is easy to see this by the way we dress. A Somali woman must cover every part of her body, except for her face, when she leaves the house. I knew that American culture was different when I came here, so I wasn't too surprised by the way the women were dressed. Some Somali women have altered their dress because of the hot weather and going to work. It is hard for me to understand how some of these women have become so easily accustomed to the American culture. It has been very hard for me to adjust to this new life. I have only been here for three months, and it is very hard.

I would like to work, but my husband says my place is in the home. Even though we could use the extra money, he does not want me to work. I studied biology in college in Somalia, but I had to quit once I got married. I would like to go to college here so that I could continue to study, but schools here are very expensive.

MUFA

INGREDIENTS: 3 cups finely ground cornmeal
1 tsp. baking powder
water

DIRECTIONS:

Mix corn flour and baking powder with water until thick. Put in a circular pan and cook at 350° until the bottom is brown and the top is soft. Goes well with soup or tea!

ADAR YUSUF ELMI

A dar Elmi arrived in Memphis in August of 1996 with four brothers and a sister. Her sentiments about cold weather reflect those of most Somalis, many of whom saw snow for the first time this past winter!

ADAR'S STORY

I like living in Memphis. It is very nice except for the cold weather! I miss my family in Somalia, but it is not a good time to be in Somalia. There is a war and people are always fighting. I don't like all the people fighting and hating each other. My husband and eight children are still in Somalia, and I worry about them a lot. Even if the war ended, I would want to stay in Memphis.

My mother taught me how to cook when I was nine. I like to cook, especially soups and bread. Finding food here is no problem.

I find all of the same things to cook with. Also, the kitchen is very similar. I cook every day. I make something different every day. A special thing I cook with is Habat Soda (literally, "black seeds"). I buy it at the Arabic grocery store and use it in teas. It tastes sweet and is used like medicine. It is believed to cure over 70 diseases!

ADAR'S RECIPES

ADAR'S FLATBREAD

INGREDIENTS:

2 cups of self-rising flour

1 egg

1 cup water

1 teaspoon corn oil

DIRECTIONS:

Preheat frying pan on medium. Mix all ingredients together. Put a little oil in the pan and spread it around. Use an ice cream scoop and pour one scoop at a time of mixture into the pan. Spread the mixture in a circular motion so it will be thin. Cook covered for 3-5 minutes. Repeat until all of the mixture has been used.

ADAR'S CHICKEN STEW

INGREDIENTS: Chicken legs

1 onion, sliced

3 carrots, washed, peeled, and sliced thin

3 red potatoes, washed, peeled, and sliced into 5-6 pieces each

1/3 cup corn oil

2 garlic cloves

1/2 can tomato sauce

1/2 cup water

1 teaspoon salt

2 chicken flavored bouillon cubes

Habat Soda*

DIRECTIONS:

Sauté carrots and onion in oil. Heat Habat Soda and garlic in a separate pan on medium heat for 5-8 minutes, then grind. Pour 4 teaspoons of water into ground mixture, then add to carrots and onion. Add tomato sauce and bring to a boil. Add the rest of the water, chicken legs, and potatoes. Cook 30 minutes, then add salt and bouillon.

COMPARATIVE AREA
Slightly larger than 1/4 the size of the United States

CLIMATE
Tropical in the south; arid desert in the north; rainy season (Apr. to Oct.)

TERRAIN
Generally flat, featureless plain; mountains in east and west.

POPULATION
Total Population – 31,547,543

0 - 14 years	– 46%
15 - 64	– 52%
65+	– 2%

LIFE EXPECTANCY

For the Total Population	– 55.12 years
Males	– 54.20 years
Females	– 56.09 years

RELIGION
Sunni Muslim (70%) in the north, indigenous beliefs 25%, Christian 5% (mostly in south and Khartoum)

LANGUAGES
Arabic (official); Nubian, Ta Bedawie; diverse dialects of Nilotic, Nilo-Hamitic, Sudanic languages; English

COMMUNICATIONS

Number of telephones	– 77,215
Number of radios	– 6.67 million
Number of televisions	– 2.06 million

MARY GENG

Mary Nyadeng Geng arrived in Memphis in August of 1995. She spoke a little English, Nuer (a tribal language of the Southern Sudanese), and a lot of Spanish! She helped us communicate with other Nuer-speaking women through an elaborate system that included two interpreters and three languages! Her Spanish was also helpful with the Cubans arriving at the time. Mary didn't have a recipe for us. Just the following story, which suggests a wisdom far beyond her years.

MARY'S STORY

Before I left Sudan, I was in a rebel prison for two months. I was in a prison because I had a political argument with the military. I kept asking them why we had to fight and go to war. I mentioned that I thought that all men should not have to be in the military and go to war if they did not desire to do so. They told me I was crazy. I just responded by saying that they were the ones who were crazy, going off to a war that solved nothing. They tried to get me to learn how to fight, but I kept telling them that I was not going to learn how to fight. I would not go off to a war that would most likely leave me for dead.

The military was very upset with me, so they put me in the rebel prison. Sometimes I got into trouble because I talked too much. They would not let me see my family at all while I was there. I almost got to the point where I would join the military so that I could just see my family. Thankfully, the mayor had come to visit the prisoners. When he came to my jail cell, he was very surprised to see me there. He knew me well, since the mayor and my father were friends. The mayor asked the people why I was there. The police who had imprisoned me told the mayor I was crazy. He would not

believe it, so he asked me what was wrong. I told him my story. After a while, the mayor told the police to set me free.

Once I was set free, the mayor told me that my mother had died. He said my family had been looking for me for days. They had no idea where I was. I was quite upset when I heard the news about my mother. I began to think my whole family was dead, since I had not seen them in months. I decided to go to a village in Kenya where an aunt of mine lived. When I arrived at her house, she thought she was seeing a ghost! My aunt had heard that I was dead! I said I was not a ghost, and that she could touch me to see that I was very much alive. My aunt began crying. She told me about my mother, too. Later on, she told me I had to leave the village because the rebels were looking for me. So I decided to go visit my father, who lived in another village. He thought I was dead, too.

My whole family thought I was dead!

When I told them what had happened, they could not believe it. I could not believe it as well! I was only 21 years old when this all happened. It is amazing how your world and life can change so quickly. After my brother heard my story, he decided to leave Sudan. He wanted to seek refuge in the U.S. My father suggested that I go with him, since he did not want my brother to be by himself. I did not want to come and leave my country and family, but my father said I should go before the rebels found me.

My brother came to Memphis first. I arrived two years later. I wanted to be with my family a while longer, since I had been away from them for so long. Before I was in prison, I had been traveling everywhere. I traveled to Uganda and to Kenya. I was in Cuba for eight years as a student. The government sends students at times to go study in different countries. I went back to my country in 1993. That is when all the trouble began. In 1995, I decided to come to Memphis to live with my brother.

I like Memphis and living in the U.S.. People actually try to help you here, and it is easier to find work. I have made good friends here. My friends and I often get together during the weekends to cook and talk. We do a lot of dancing, too. It is an all day event when we get together.

Another good thing about living in the U.S. is that there is much more freedom. Women from my country do not have much freedom. The role of Sudanese women is to take care of the Sudanese men. The women should be good wives and mothers. Also, the Sudanese man is allowed to have as many wives as he likes, but the woman is not allowed to have more than one husband. There is just no equality between the sexes!

I do, however, want to go back to Sudan to be with my family. I plan to go back in three years, after I have saved some money. Even though there is still a war going on, I miss my family a lot and want to be with them. I have 47 siblings. Most of them are from different wives of my father's. Even though my actual mother is dead, I have five other mothers through my father's other marriages. I call them all "mother," too. We never call them by their actual names. Some people find it hard to believe that I know all the names of my siblings, but if you have lived with them all your life, you have to know them pretty well. In Sudan, all families live close together. It is like a village, since a typical Sudanese family is rather large.

The dinners in my family were a huge event. No matter what, we would always eat together as a family. For dinners, we usually had two people who would cook the meal. My mother used to do a lot of cooking. She taught me how to cook before she died. My mother wanted me to learn how to cook so I could be ready when I was married. When a woman is married, no one can cook for her. The woman must do everything. It is something we are taught from birth.

MARY MOGGA

Mary Mogga came to Memphis in September of 1994 with her five children. She is now working with Tennessee State University Agricultural Extension Service. this summer, she is helping Refugee Services with a community gardening project for refugee families.

MARY'S STORY

The first civil war in Sudan was from 1955-1972. I lived in Uganda for nine years with my family as a refugee. Uganda was a British colony, so I was able to learn English in primary school. During a period of relative peace in Sudan, my family got repatriated back to Sudan. I continued my junior high and high school education in southern Sudan at the English Pattern School. I was lucky because my father valued education. I was allowed to go to school, unlike most girls in Sudan. I also went to college and received a degree in General Tropical Agriculture. For 10 years, I worked as Research Officer for the World Bank's Agricultural Research Project. While working for the World Bank, I was sent for training in Britain at Reading University. I studied Field Crop Experimentation for 11 months.

I had to leave Sudan again when the war broke out. My husband was a director with the Ministry of Finance. The taxation department strongly opposed the government's policies. I had some problems with the Islamic Organization that was rationing food to convert women to Islam. I created a women's coalition through the Episcopal Church, where my late father was the archdeacon. I escaped and lived in Kenya for three years at a refugee camp. While there, I advocated for the educational needs of the southern Sudanese women in exile. I received a grant from the Hugh Pilkington Charitable Trust. Oxfam-UK then offered me a job as Program Officer for Relief and Rehabilitation Projects for refugees and displaced people at the camps. I did mostly income-generating projects with the women, like vegetable production, grinding mills, and poultry and goat raising. While in Oxfam, I was sent to Britain to do post-graduate work in Women's Rural Extension. I made excellent grades and was offered a full scholarship to complete my master's. However, I had to return to Kenya because I had a contract with Oxfam.

I have been in Memphis for three years. I still have contact with my director at Oxfam. She informs me that my projects are still going. I am very proud of this. In September, I will receive my travel visa. I hope to go back to Britain and meet up with my teachers. Ultimately, I would like to organize refugee women here in Memphis. I want the women to learn how to help themselves. Sudan is a patriarchal society in which women have very little freedom. Women in America have freedom of choice in all arenas—social, economic, and political.

Several things have been hard for me to adjust to here. American English and slang are very different from the British English that I learned in school. I am also not used to the disrespectful attitudes of students towards their teachers, especially in high school. My children are traumatized by this. It also upsets me that children here are allowed to date when they are only twelve. I am nervous about my children's future.

When I first arrived, I was very confused by the bus system. My second day in Memphis, I got on a bus and sat down in the back. I was waiting for someone to come sell me a ticket, like in England. The driver started yelling at me, and I didn't understand why. A person sitting next to me explained that I had to pay first. I only had a ten dollar bill. The driver said I had to have exact change and kept the whole ten dollars!

I miss Sudan, especially my extended family and the food. My mother taught me how to cook when I was nine years old. In my culture, women are caregivers and must know how to cook. I make traditional food at home, but it isn't the same. I like some American food. Barbecue is my favorite. For big celebrations in Sudan, like marriages and births, we slaughter a ram or a goat. We eat the meat with traditional beans and vegetables.

MARY TELLS ABOUT COWPEAS!

Cowpeas are used in the traditional baby naming ceremony by particular ethnic groups in Sudan. The naming ceremony is four to seven days after the baby is born. (It is held whenever the baby's umbilical cord falls off.) Cowpeas are a symbol of peace, because they are bland and everyone likes to eat them. At the baby naming ceremony, the baby's body is covered with a special mixture of sesame seeds, oil, and a red mineral. It is very soothing for the baby's skin. Lactating women eat cowpeas at the ceremony so their milk will be nutritious.

This tradition is dying out now that Christianity has come to Sudan, and people are becoming more educated. However, the traditional ceremony is still being practiced in conjunction with a big meal or feast.

MARY'S RECIPES

OKRA BEEF STEW

INGREDIENTS:

1 lb. cubed beef

2 cups cut okra

2 onions, chopped

2 tablespoons sesame oil

1/2 small can of tomato paste

3 - 4 garlic cloves, chopped

Cinnamon, cumin, salt, and pepper to taste

Pinch of sugar

DIRECTIONS:

Sauté onions in sesame oil, then add beef and okra. Add tomato paste and other spices. Stir until the meat is cooked. Serve with bread or rice.

COWPEAS

INGREDIENTS:

2 cups of cowpeas (kidney beans or pinto beans may be used)

Pinch of sodium bicarbonate

1 tablespoon sesame butter*

1 tablespoon peanut butter

DIRECTIONS:

Boil the cowpeas in enough water to cover them. Add the pinch of sodium bicarbonate, the sesame butter and the peanut butter. Slow cook the beans and stir frequently to keep the oil on top.

LENTILS

INGREDIENTS:

2 cups lentils, boiled and mashed

1 onion, grated

2 -3 cloves of garlic, pounded

Parsley, cinnamon, cloves, cardamom, black pepper, and salt to taste

Pinch of sugar

DIRECTIONS:

Sauté onion and garlic, add other spices and combine with the cooked lentils.

Sarah Loang, Nyakir Pal, Buk Roam, and Nyadeng Ter are all members of a special ESL (English as a Second Language) class for Sudanese women taught by volunteers at Refugee Services. They shared these comments and recipes in an interview conducted during their class.

THEIR STORY

We learned to cook as small children from our mothers and grandmothers. Cooking is a woman's job. We are always in the kitchen! Sometimes a man knows how to cook, but not often. In Sudan, the kitchens are outside, and we cooked with a fire on the ground. In America, we use an indoor kitchen, of course. We use pots and pans and the stove and oven.

We can find most of the foods here that we grew up eating, like rice, noodles, flour, bread, beans, and vegetables. We can find everything at Kroger, Piggly Wiggly, Megamarket. We don't

LEFT TO RIGHT: Nyadeng Ter, Sarah Loang, Nyanyual Duoth, Nyadeng Tual, Nyadeng Yiech, Nyakir Pal, Buk Roam, Nyaluak Bol Tut

shop at a special grocery store. We do miss special sauces and hot peppers. In the refugee camp, we mostly cooked beans and rice. We got it in big bags, and it was easy to make because we just added oil and water.

In America, women have much more freedom. They have friends, go to school, and get jobs. In Sudan, a woman only has her husband and many babies. American women don't have to worry about their husbands and children all the time. Women here get to have a fuller life. Also women have boyfriends! In Sudan women are married and that's it.

CATFISH

INGREDIENTS:
Catfish, cut into 1" pieces
1 onion, chopped
3 cups water
1 tablespoon butter
Juice of 1/2 lemon
3 cloves garlic, crushed
Salt and pepper to taste

DIRECTIONS:
Clean and wash the catfish, remove bones, and cut into small pieces. Put fish and chopped onion in a large pot. Add water, butter, lemon juice, and pepper. In a small bowl, mash garlic and salt together, then add to fish. Turn burner on high until mixture comes to a boil, then let simmer for 30 minutes. Serve with rice.

SLAW

INGREDIENTS:
1/2 head of green cabbage, shredded
1 medium tomato, chopped
1 small onion, chopped
1 teaspoon salt
2 teaspoons vinegar

DIRECTIONS:
Combine ingredients in a large bowl and mix.

THE MIDDLE EAST

It is almost impossible to get through a day without hearing some news, good or bad, about the latest happenings in the Middle East. The Gulf War brought Refugee Services our first large group of people from this part of the world—Iraqis—who began arriving in 1991, at the end of that war. For our staff, the conflict in the Middle East suddenly moved off of the TV screen and into our lives, as we welcomed more and more people who were forced to flee the horror perpetrated on his own people by Saddam Hussein.

The number of Iraqis coming to Memphis have increased little by little since the end of the Gulf War, with the number of new arrivals last year reaching seventy-eight. These refugees from **IRAQ** have spent years in refugee camps in Saudi Arabia, waiting for their chance at freedom.

Last fall, we welcomed a new population from a part of the Middle East known as Kurdistan. The Kurds were airlifted to safety on Guam by our military after they were attacked by Saddam Hussein's forces.   The Kurds have been struggling for centuries for a land of their own, **KURDISTAN**, which would include parts of what is now Iraq, Iran, Turkey, and Syria. With the arrival of another group of Kurds this spring, a new community is beginning here in Memphis. We are pleased to bring you the recipes and stories of some of the women of the Memphis Middle Eastern community.

COMPARATIVE AREA

Slightly more than twice the area of Idaho

CLIMATE

Mostly desert; mild to cool winters with dry, hot, cloudless summers; northern mountainous regions (KURDISTAN) along Iranian and Turkish borders experience cold winters with occasionally heavy snows which melt in early spring, sometimes causing extensive flooding in central southern Iraq.

TERRAIN

Mostly broad plains; reedy marshes along Iranian border in south; mountains along borders with Iran and Turkey (KURDISTAN).

POPULATION

Total Population – 21,422,292
0 - 14 years	– 48%
15 - 64	– 49%
65+	– 3%

LIFE EXPECTANCY

For the Total Population	– 66.95 years
Males	– 65.92 years
Females	– 68.03 years

RELIGION

Muslim 97% (Shi'a 60-65%, Sunni 32-37%), Christian or other 3%

LANGUAGES

Arabic, Kurdish (official language in Kurdish regions), Assyrian, Armenian

COMMUNICATIONS

Number of telephones	–632,000
Number of radios	– 4.02 million
Number of televisions	– 1 million

AMINA AL-CHOKHACHI

Amina Al-Chokhachi is originally from Iraq. Her first stay in Memphis was in the 1960's, when she received training as a pharmacist at the University of Tennessee. She is back here now with her family, using her language skills and her medical training to help newly arriving refugees from all over the world.

AMINA'S STORY

My mother taught me how to cook. Most of the recipes I know have been passed down from generation to generation. There are many recipes, however, that I know that come from different parts of the country. Iraq has had many different influences from other countries, such as Lebanon and Iran. The different cultures can be seen in some of the recipes we cook. For example, there are many Iraqi dishes that have rice, which came from the Iranian idea of food centering around rice. The use of rice is known to be the sun around which satellite dishes revolve and interplay. It has become part of our culture, because our grandmothers and ancestors learned how to cook these recipes.

The family dinner in Iraq is somewhat different than it is here in the U.S.. In Iraq, one never actually sits down around a table for dinner. The table is always full of dishes, so all we do is fill up our plates and find somewhere else around the house to sit down. The one main difference with dinner between the U.S. and Iraq is that a person has to have an afternoon tea invitation. The invitation would eventually lead into lunch or dinner.

It is mostly women who prepare the dishes. The men help only when the meal will be a big occasion, and the women need help moving heavy objects. It takes a lot of work to prepare meals during special holidays such as Ramadan. Even though this is a time when we fast, we have to prepare special meals so that after sunset we can eat food to energize our bodies. I enjoy these times, because family and friends come together and actually eat together. We all try to visit one another during these times, too.

Holidays such as Ramadan make me realize how much I miss my family. Most of my family is still in Iraq. I want so desperately for all our family to be safe and together. I just wish our country could reach some type of normality. Even though we do not have most of the family here, we do make the effort to get together. We try to prepare as many dinners as we can, so that those of us who are here in the U.S. can be together. We love to be around each other, especially during the evening and at religious ceremonies. The times we have together are not taken for granted.

AMINA TELLS ABOUT RAMADAN

Ramadan is one of the holiest months for Muslims. All Muslims nine years old and older are required to fast. Fasting is not just a matter of not eating or drinking. Fasting is a way of testing people. It tests how much they do towards God and to themselves and towards other people. Ramadan falls during one of the lunar months. It begins when the moon shows and lasts 28 or 29 days. Ramadan is the ninth month, according to the Islamic calendar.

I have been fasting since I was nine years old. I have seen all of my family and those in my surroundings fast my whole life. I grew up in this environment. Everybody fasts, except for those who are really sick. God forgives the sick. He says a person should not hurt himself by fasting. Especially people with chronic diseases like diabetes and high blood pressure. These people do not fast, but they give some of their money to the poor. If a healthy person does not fast for a day or two because of a minor illness, he tries to replace the day he did not fast during the year before the next Ramadan. Fasting means not eating or drinking any kind of food or drink, even water, from sunrise until sunset. When I fast all day, I feel like making all kinds of foods! I cook so much food that my family can't eat it all!

A special thing about Ramadan is that I feel different during the month. I have completely different feelings deep inside. If I see an enemy, I feel so much like asking for forgiveness. It is important just to reconcile and forget about whatever happened. If I don't have an enemy, I may even feel like helping two other enemies reconcile their differences. And this I feel has a lot to do with God's love. Mostly, I can see people reading the Koran during Ramadan. The more I read it, the more feelings I have towards God.

When Ramadan ends, we have a feast. The feast is three days long. It is called *Al Fatr*, which means "break the fasting." Each day during Ramadan, when the sun sets, we say "fatr," which means it is time to eat. At the end of the month, when it is possible to see the moon, the next day is the end. During Ramadan, you see people getting together a lot, visiting each other, spending a lot of time at the mosque, and cooking certain kinds of foods, for example sweets, like baklava. Families have everybody sitting at the table eating together, which is nice. Back home, men and women go to the mosque together and pray in a big group. People see friends that they haven't seen in a long time. This is the time for everyone to get together and forget about work and other things. We exchange gifts, such as a new outfit. Almost everyone tries to wear a new outfit. The children enjoy the celebration. They go to the playground and travel around visiting others.

AMINA'S RECIPES

AMINA'S BAKLAVA

INGREDIENTS:
- 1 1/2 boxes filo dough
- 1 lb. chopped walnuts
- 1/2 cup sugar
- 2/3 cup confectioner's sugar
- 3/4 teaspoon cinnamon
- 2 teaspoons rose water*
- 1 lb. melted, unsalted butter

Syrup:
- 2 cups sugar
- 1 1/2 cups water
- Dash of cinnamon
- 3 teaspoons lemon juice
- 3 teaspoons rose water

TABOULI

INGREDIENTS:
- I cup cracked wheat
- 2 bunches of parsley, finely chopped
- 1 bunch of cilantro, finely chopped
- 1 tomato, finely chopped
- 5 green onions, finely chopped
- Juice of two or more lemons
- 4 teaspoons olive oil
- Salt and pepper to taste

DIRECTIONS:

Mix syrup ingredients in a saucepan and bring to a slow boil. Cook for about 45 minutes or until it resembles a soft ball.

Thaw filo dough 2 hours before using. Mix walnuts with both sugars, cinnamon, and rose water. Spread the melted butter on tray, then lay 20 layers of dough, spreading each layer with butter. Work quickly so it doesn't dry out. Spread the nut mixture. Continue layering the rest of the dough, spreading each with butter until all of the layers have been used. Cut into diamond shapes or square pieces. Brush top with butter.

Bake at 300° for one hour, or until it becomes light brown. Pour syrup on top while hot.

DIRECTIONS:

Soak cracked wheat until it becomes soft. Combine parsley, cilantro, tomato, and onion, then add drained, cracked wheat. Season with olive oil, lemon juice, salt and pepper.

*T*rudy Al-Chokhachi, a native-born American, is Amina's aunt. She has been married to Amina's uncle for over 35 years. She met him in Knoxville while he was in school there. She lived for three years in Iraq, where she came to learn about and love Iraqi cooking.

TRUDY'S RECIPES

GROUND MEAT KABOBS

INGREDIENTS:
1 lb. lean ground beef
1/4 cup fresh parsley
1 medium grated onion
1 teaspoon black pepper
1 teaspoon salt

DIRECTIONS:

Combine all ingredients in a large bowl. Mix well. Let stand for 30 minutes in the refrigerator. Using about 1/4 cup of the mixture for each kabob, shape around metal or wooden skewers. Moistening your hands will help mold the meat mixture. Place over hot coals, turning frequently, until meat is cooked as desired.

LIMA BEAN RICE

INGREDIENTS:
3 cups uncooked rice
6 cups water
1 lb. stew meat
1 lb. bag of lima beans
1 big bunch of fresh dillweed, chopped
4 -5 tablespoons vegetable oil
Salt to taste

DIRECTIONS:

Sauté the meat for 10 minutes in a saucepan, then add 6 cups of water. Let it cook until the meat is done. Save 4 cups of the broth. In a separate saucepan, sauté the lima beans and chopped dillweed for 5 minutes. Then add the meat and the four cups of broth. Bring to a boil and add salt. Rinse rice in cold water. Drain the rice, then add it to the mixture. Cover and cook for 10-15 minutes on medium heat. Then simmer for 10-15 minutes on low heat. Serve warm.

N azek Al-Rufui has been living in the U.S. for about ten years now. Amina says she's an excellent cook, and knows how to fix dishes from all over the Middle East.

NAZEK'S RECIPES

EGGPLANT KABOBS

INGREDIENTS:

2 large eggplants
1 lb. ground beef
8 oz. tomato sauce
Vegetable oil
Lemon juice
1/2 teaspoon garlic powder
One bunch chopped parsley
1/2 teaspoon salt
1/2 teaspoon pepper

DIRECTIONS:

Slice eggplant vertically into 1/2" slices. Place in salt water for half an hour. Remove and dry with a paper towel. Fry eggplant in oil until both sides turn golden brown. Set aside to cool.

Mix meat, salt, pepper, and garlic powder together. Take small pieces of the mixture and shape into finger sized hot dogs. Fry until thoroughly cooked. Set aside to cool.

Wrap each kabob with a slice of eggplant. Put into a 8x12 baking dish at least 2" deep. Combine tomato sauce and a cup of water and pour evenly over it. Add salt and lemon juice to taste. Cover with foil and bake 30 minutes at 350°. Remove from oven and garnish with chopped parsley. Serve hot with rice.

STEAMED SAFFRON RICE

INGREDIENTS:

4 cups lightly salted water
2 cups long grain rice
1 teaspoons butter or margarine
1/2 teaspoon saffron*
Salt to taste

DIRECTIONS:

Bring water and saffron to boil in a large pot. Add rice. Water should cover rice by two inches or more. Cook uncovered over medium heat for 7 to 10 minutes. Reduce heat and place a clean towel over the rice. Cook like this for 25 - 30 minutes or until rice is fluffy and water is absorbed. Keep covered until ready to serve.

GOLALA NOORI ROSTAM

G olala Noori came to the United States in the spring of 1997. In this interview, she shares her strong longing for home as well as her favorite recipes. Her words are a striking reminder that many refugees flee for their lives, and that the choice to do so is often a difficult one, sometimes questioned during the first few difficult months of resettlement.

GOLALA'S STORY

M y family and I have been here for 25 days. So far, I do not like living in Memphis. We left everything back in our country—our family, houses, and friends. We actually had transportation to go to and from places. We did not have to walk everywhere like we do here. I also left a good job. I was a high school economics teacher in Kurdistan. I am not sure whether or not I would like to teach here. My English is not that good yet. I do not think teaching here would be the same as it was in Kurdistan. Everyone there studies English in high school. I have spoken it for a few years, but I do not feel I can speak it well.

It would be easier for me to go back to Kurdistan. I miss

everything. I miss not being able to go out into my neighborhood to visit with family and friends. Also, I miss the picnics. In Kurdistan, we always went on picnics. It was such a fun time to be with family and friends. Hopefully, I will be able to adjust to the lifestyle here. I realize that my family and I have only been here a few days, but the American lifestyle is a little different. The way Americans dress is different. For example, Kurdish

women do not wear short skirts like I have seen American women wear. We also do not have boyfriends and girlfriends as the Americans do. One reason for that is our religion does not allow it. From elementary to high school, the boys and girls go to separate schools. Sometimes the parents arrange for their child to meet a hopeful marriage partner, but it is the person's own decision whom they choose to marry. There is not really any dating. A Kurdish man or woman just sees the person they would like to marry. The legal age for Kurdish people to get married is twenty. Most Kurds get married between the ages of twenty and twenty-five. I was married when I was 20 years old. My son is eighteen. So he may be married in two years. My son, however, does not think so!

Kurdish men can marry more than one woman. Our prophet, Mohammed, had seven wives. A man can marry four women. None of the married men here in Memphis have more than one wife. How many wives a man has depends greatly on how wealthy he is. If the man has a lot of money, then he can afford to have another wife. It is very expensive to have more than one wife.

The Kurdistan wedding is not very different from the American wedding. We also have the exchange of rings and a reception afterwards. A priest, however, does not perform the marriage ceremony. The couple gets a chief of the court, who is referred to as Imam.

The younger Kurdish women do not cover their faces as the older women do. It is in Iran where it is mandatory that all women cover part of their face. There is a difference in religion between the Kurds and the Iranians. We are both Muslim countries, but there are two different types of Muslims, Shiite and Sunni. The Iranians are Shiite, which isa little bit stricter.

Kurdish food is very different from American food. My family and I have not been to a restaurant to eat, but I have had American food such as pizza and hamburger. Kurdistan has pizza that is just like American pizza.

I think it is harder to cook and prepare Kurdish food. It has not been difficult to find the food that we need to prepare a meal, though. We have to go to the grocery store every day. Our refrigerator cannot hold all the food that I

buy for my family. In Kurdistan, I bought food for a whole month. Now, I send my children to the grocery store almost every day.

It is typically the Kurdish women who prepare the meals. The men never cook. It is rare to find a Kurdish man who cooks. I ask my boys to help me sometimes. They usually help me clean the kitchen.

The very big and important meals for us take place during and after Ramadan. During Ramadan, we fast until sunset. The food that we eat during this religious holiday has to be filling, since we will not get to eat until the next sunset. For the Kurdish people, the feast that takes place three days after Ramadan is called Jazhny Ramadan. We also have another feast called Jazhny Qurban that takes place seventy days after Ramadan. This is one of the biggest feasts. It is like a huge and long party that we celebrate with many families and friends.

YAPRAKH
(STUFFED ONION, POTATO, AND CABBAGE CASSEROLE)

INGREDIENTS:
- I head of cabbage
- 1 onion
- 4 - 5 small red potatoes
- 1 tablespoon olive oil

DIRECTIONS:

Put the cabbage in boiling water until it softens and leaves peel off easily.

Cut ends off of the onion and remove the outer skin. Cut the onion from the side to the middle. Take the middle part out and chop it. Drop the rest of the onion in boiling water until it softens and easily peels off in layers.

Filling Ingredients:
- 1lb. ground beef
- 1/2 cup uncooked rice
- 6-oz. can tomato paste
- 1/2 bunch chopped parsley
- 1/2 teaspoon curry powder
- 1 tablespoon lemon juice
- Salt to taste

In a large bowl mix the rice, ground beef, chopped parsley, chopped onion, tomato paste, salt and curry powder.

Grease pot with oil. Cut each potato in half, remove insides, and fill with stuffing, then put back together and place in bottom of the pot.

Put 1 -2 tablespoons of stuffing in each onion peel and roll it up. Then arrange in the bottom of the pot. Do the same with the cabbage and arrange them on top of the onions.

Add water until it is just below the top row of the stuffed cabbage. Add lemon juice. Put a heavy plate on top of the stuffed cabbage (not the cover) and cook on high until water boils off (about 30 minutes). When done cooking, put a platter on top of the pot and flip over so that the onion is on top. Serve.

KUFFTA (STUFFED RICE ROLLS)

FILLING INGREDIENTS:
1 onion, chopped
1 lb. ground beef
1/2 cup raisins
1/2 cup chopped almonds
1/4 teaspoon allspice
1/4 teaspoon curry powder
1/4 teaspoon lemon juice

WRAPPER INGREDIENTS:
2 cups cooked rice
1 small boiled potato
1 egg
1/4 teaspoon turmeric
Salt to taste

DIRECTIONS:

Combine ingredients for the filling and cook until meat is brown. Set aside.

Combine ingredients for the wrapper and mash well. Divide into small patties (about 2"). Put 1 tablespoon of filling in each and enclose. Deep fry. For best results, freeze before deep frying.

SHIFTA (KURDISH HAMBURGER)

INGREDIENTS:
1 lb. uncooked ground beef
1 onion, chopped
1 tomato, diced
1 cup flour
2 - 3 cloves garlic, chopped
1/2 cup celery leaves, chopped
1/2 teaspoon curry powder
1 egg

DIRECTIONS:

Combine ingredients with hands and form into long oval patties. Cook in a pan on medium heat until browned all the way through.

BRIANY (KURDISH-STYLE RICE)

INGREDIENTS:
    1 cup of rice
    1/4 cup split peas
    1 lb. ground beef
    1 chicken breast, chopped
    2 carrots, chopped
    1 onion, chopped
    2 red potatoes, chopped
    1 teaspoon curry powder

DIRECTIONS:

Boil rice and split peas in water until cooked. Combine other ingredients and pan fry until done. Mix with rice and peas and serve.

KURDISH BREAD

INGREDIENTS:
    1 cup self-rising flour
    Water to moisten
    Salt to taste

DIRECTIONS:

Mix ingredients well and knead for 5-10 minutes. Roll dough out as flat as possible and bake.

PARDA PLOW

DIRECTIONS:

Wrap Briany in Kurdish Bread dough and bake for 30 minutes.

BAHAR HASSAN

*B*ahar Hassan came with her family to Memphis in November of 1996. Like many other refugees, she is struggling with the loss of her profession and the problems created by the ever-present language barrier in her new home.

BAHAR'S STORY

I've been here about three months. I like Memphis, but I don't get to do very much. One time I went to the zoo, and that was nice. In Kurdistan, there is lots of open space. My favorite thing to do is go on a picnic. March 21st is the Kurdish celebration Newroz. It is also the first day of spring. We celebrate by going out to the park for a picnic. We also wear traditional dresses and dance.

When I think about my future here, I don't know. I must learn English better. If I learn English, I can become a teacher. In Kurdistan, I was a teacher. Here, I am a student!

I learned to cook when I was twelve. I enjoy cooking. I like everything about it. I make bread every morning so that it is ready for dinner. Usually, for breakfast we eat cheese and bread. Lunch and dinner are usually soup, rice, and chicken. I haven't tried much American food, but I like pizza. I even learned how to make it!

BAHAR'S RECIPE

TAHCHINE (RAISIN-ALMOND RICE)

INGREDIENTS:

2 cups basmati rice*
3 1/2 cups water
2 tablespoons canola oil
1/4 teaspoon turmeric
1 small potato chopped into bite-size pieces
1/2 cup raisins

1/2 cup chopped almonds
Salt, allspice, curry powder, lemon juice to taste

DIRECTIONS:

Combine rice, water, turmeric, and salt and cook on high until rice is done. In a separate pan, fry potatoes in oil until crispy, then add raisins and almonds. Serve on top of rice.

BOSNIA

The history of the war in the Balkans is a complicated one, based on ethnic and religious rivalries that stretch far back in time. Like many Americans during the War Between The States, people in this part of the world have found themselves suddenly fighting neighbors who, only days before, worked beside them in the fields. The region still struggles for peace, and American troops are actively involved in this struggle. Americans here in the States are also actively involved through the resettlement efforts of many programs such as ours.

COMPARATIVE AREA

Slightly smaller than West Virginia

CLIMATE

Hot summers and cold winters; areas of high elevation have short, cool summers and long, severe winters; mild, rainy winters along the coast.

TERRAIN

Mountains and valleys

POPULATION

Total Population – 2,656,240

0 - 14 years	*– 20%*
15 - 64	*– 68%*
65+	*– 12%*

LIFE EXPECTANCY

For the Total Population	*– 56.11 years*
Males	*– 51.16 years*
Females	*– 61.39 years*

RELIGION

Muslim 40%, Orthodox 31%, Catholic 15%, Protestant 4%, other 10%

LANGUAGES

Serbo-Croatian 99%

COMMUNICATIONS

Number of telephones	*– 727,000*
Number of radios	*– 840,000*
Number of televisions	*– 1,012,074*

BOSNIA

MIRA BAKALOVIC

Mira Bakalovic came to Memphis in May of 1995. Although her children were here in the States, Mira began her new life in America alone, and she has worked very hard to improve her English skills and to support herself outside of the profession in which she was trained in Bosnia. Although she didn't share a recipe, she did talk with us a little, and sadly, about her new life in Memphis and the war back home.

MIRA'S STORY

Bosnia is a very interesting country. I truly miss my country. Unfortunately, I have not been very happy living here in Memphis. It has been sad for me. I was very independent in Bosnia. I had a great job and could move around more easily. I was an architect before I moved here. I have been taking computer lessons for a few months so that I can climb up the career ladder more easily, but it has been hard. Since I speak very little English, it is hard for me to move around the city and find a good-paying job. It is very hard adjusting to a lifestyle that is so different from the one I had in Bosnia.

The war in Bosnia has changed everything. My beautiful country is being destroyed by bombs. Part of my apartment was blown away by a bomb. Because of the war, many Bosnians are leaving the country. It is not a safe place to live anymore. There are many people being killed, innocent people. I feel so sorry for the children that are living in such a violent world. I am afraid for how these children will grow up.

The cooking style here is not very different from in Bosnia. The Bosnian kitchen is very similar to the one here. The food is a little different. Bosnians love eating veal and lamb. During El Hadj, lamb is always prepared. People go out into the garden or forest to celebrate the holiday with family, and then roast the lamb. There are many different holidays in Bosnia, since there are many different religions. We celebrate our Independence Day on July 4th, too!

Bosnians prepare many pie dishes of meat, cheese, or spinach. While my children lived in Little Rock as exchange students, I sent their host family a pie made with cheese and ground meat. The family loved it!

DINA PLACO

*D*ina Placo arrived in Memphis with her husband in August of 1994. She and her husband have two sons born since their arrival, and they are excellent examples of families who, through courage and determination, go about the work of successfully starting over.

DINA'S STORY

I have lived in Memphis now for two and a half years. The short time that I have been living here, I have tried to help other Bosnians adjust to their new life. I have been helping many families by cooking or going to the grocery store. There is this one family who has a son in the hospital that I have visited quite often. I try to help the mother by cooking, running errands for her, and clarifying hospital information. I enjoy helping others a lot.

The Bosnian woman is not very different from the American woman. Bosnian women are very independent. Of course, the better educated she is, the more independence and opportunities the woman will have. I went to school to study geology before I moved to Memphis. I never had a chance, however, to work as a geologist. Soon after I graduated from college, my husband and I sought refuge in Memphis. Then I became pregnant with the first of my two sons. At the moment, I work in the bakery at Seessel's. I enjoy working there, but I know that I am not going to be working there forever. I hope to go to school here and continue my education.

Life before the war was very different. One did not have to worry about death and see violence out in the streets. I was in high school before the war started. I remember working for my father during the summer so that I could have some extra money. My father had a small company that repaired air conditioners. My youngest sister is now in high school. She, unfortunately, has had to learn to adjust to living through a war. I am sure it is hard to be a teenager, worrying constantly about death and violence.

I like living in Memphis. Even though I am away from most of my family, I feel much safer here than in Bosnia. It was hard living here at first, because we did not have much. Things have improved with time, and I know that they will get better. I hope to have a house and not live in an apartment any longer. My family will need a bigger place so that my sons can move around more. Also, when we have friends and family over for dinner, there is barely enough room for all the food and people!

HADJESKI CHEVAP
(BOSNIAN-STYLE STEW)

INGREDIENTS:
1 1/2 lbs. veal or beef, sliced
1 large onion, chopped
2 cans mushrooms, sliced
4 medium tomatoes
8 oz. can of tomato sauce
1 stick butter
1 teaspoon chopped parsley
Salt and pepper to taste

DIRECTIONS:
Brown meat and 1/2 stick of butter in a pan on high, then remove from heat. In a separate pot, boil water, then add tomatoes. Remove after a few minutes. Core and peel. Chop tomatoes and add to tomato sauce. Cook mushrooms and onion on low heat with 1/2 stick of butter. After 10 minutes, add tomato mixture, salt, pepper, and parsley. Line a pan with foil, then add meat and vegetable sauce, cover the top with foil, and bake at 300° for 30 minutes. Serve hot.

BUREK
(CURLED MEAT DUMPLINGS)

INGREDIENTS:
1 lb. flour
2 teaspoons salt
1 tablespoon oil

DIRECTIONS:
Combine ingredients and add enough water to soften. Knead for 20 minutes and then separate into four balls. Roll each ball out like a snake and flatten.

FILLING INGREDIENTS:
1 lb. ground beef
1 medium onion, chopped
1/2 teaspoon black pepper
1 teaspoon salt

DIRECTIONS:
Cook meat with onion, salt, and pepper. Then put filling along the rolled out dough and enclose. Shape into coils and place in a greased baking pan with 8 oz. of water. Cook at 350° for 45 minutes.

STRUDEL

INGREDIENTS:

(A) 3 eggs, 1/2 cup sugar, 1 stick melted butter

(B) 8 oz. milk, 1 tablespoon yeast, 1 tablespoon flour, 1 tablespoon sugar

(C) 2 cups of flour, 1 teaspoon salt

(D) 1 tablespoon rum flavoring, 15 oz. raisins, 3 eggs, 1 cup sugar, 1 stick butter

DIRECTIONS:

Combine group (A). In a separate bowl, combine group (B). Let stand for 20 minutes, then combine (B) with (A) and (C). Set aside and wait for mixture to double in size. Divide the dough into two pieces. Combine group (D) and brush over dough, then roll up and bake at 350° for 45 minutes.

NABUJK (PASTA CASSEROLE)

INGREDIENTS:

3/4 lb. pasta (macaroni, spirals, or shells), cooked
1 bunch broccoli, chopped and boiled
3 eggs
1/2 pint whipping cream
1 teaspoon salt
1/2 teaspoon white pepper
1 cup grated mozzarella cheese
1 teaspoon oregano

DIRECTIONS:

In a greased 8"x12" baking dish, alternate layers of broccoli and pasta. Combine eggs, whipping cream, salt and pepper, and pour over the top. Next, sprinkle on the cheese. Add the oregano. Bake at 350° for 30 minutes.

APPENDICES

UNITED STATES STATISTICS

COMPARATIVE AREA

About three-tenths the size of Africa

CLIMATE

Mostly temperate, but tropical in Hawaii and Florida and arctic in Alaska, semi-arid in the Great Plains, west of the Mississippi River and arid in the Great Basin of the southwest; low winter temperatures in the northwest are ameliorated in January and Feburary by warm Shinook winds from the eastern slopes of the Rocky Mountains.

TERRAIN

Vast central plain, mountains in west, hills and low mountains in east; rugged mountains and broad river valleys in Alaska; rugged, volcanic typography in Hawaii.

POPULATION

Total Population – 226,476,278

0 - 14 years	*– 22%*
15 - 64	*– 65%*
65+	*– 13%*

LIFE EXPECTANCY

For the Total Population	*– 75.95 years*
Males	*– 72.65 years*
Females	*– 79.41 years*

RELIGION

Protestant 56%, Roman Catholic 28%, Jewish 2%, Other 4%, and None 10%.

LANGUAGES

English, Spanish (spoken by a sizeable minority)

COMMUNICATIONS

Number of telephones	*– 182.558 million*
Number of radios	*– 540.5 million*
Number of televisions	*– 215 million*

REFUGEES ARRIVING IN MEMPHIS

COUNTRY	1994	1995	1996	TOTALS
BOSNIA	13	14	78	35
CUBA	—	220	12	232
HAITI	32	—	—	32
IRAQ	55	32	8	165
SOMALIA	42	49	141	232
SUDAN	20	39	—	59
VIETNAM	168	152	88	408
TOTALS	**330**	**506**	**327**	**1,163**

INTERNATIONAL GROCERY STORES

NAME OF GROCERY	ADDRESS	PHONE	TYPE OF MARKET
Asian Groceries	5054 American Way	368-0068	Asian & Indian
Cynthia's Latin Market	3935 Summer Avenue	458-9639	Latin
Emilio's Grocery	2757 Getwell	365-3015	Latin
International Food Market	3925 Barron	452-8505	Middle Eastern
Mediterranean Grocery	620 South Highland	320-5757	Middle Eastern
Mercado Latino	4118 Jackson	385-7667	Latin
My Thanh Oriental Market	304 North Cleveland	725-5079	Asian
New Asian Food Company	414 North Cleveland	725-5079	Asian
Oriental Best Food Store	3731 South Mendenhall	366-1570	Asian
Oriental Center Park & Shop	3664 Summer Avenue	327-9756	Asian
Sam's Oriental Grocery	758 Mt. Moriah	682-3569	Asian
Sang Express	1277 South Wellington	942-5749	Asian
Wild Oats	5101 Sanderlin	685-2293	Variety
Wild Oats	1801 Union	725-4823	Variety

INDICES

THE WOMEN

THE RECIPES

SOUPS AND STEWS

MEATS AND POULTRY

FISH AND SEAFOOD

SALADS

SAUCES

VEGETARIAN

BREADS AND DESSERTS